the ZERO-WASTE CHEF

the ZERO-WASTE CHEF

Plant-Forward Recipes and Tips for a Sustainable Kitchen and Planet

ANNE-MARIE BONNEAU

AVERY
an imprint of Penguin Random House
New York

an imprint of Penguin Random House LLC
penguinrandomhouse.com

Most Avery books are available at special quantity discounts for bulk purchase
for sales promotions, premiums, fund-raising, and educational needs.
Special books or book excerpts also can be created to fit specific needs.
For details, write SpecialMarkets@penguinrandomhouse.com.

Library of Congress Cataloging-in-Publication Data

Names: Bonneau, Anne Marie, author.
Title: The zero-waste chef: plant-forward recipes and tips for a sustainable
kitchen and planet / Anne-Marie Bonneau.
Description: New York: Avery, an imprint of Penguin Random House,
[2021] | Includes index.
Identifiers: LCCN 2020025732 (print) | LCCN 2020025733 (ebook) |
ISBN 9780593188774 (paperback) | ISBN 9780593188781 (ebook)
Subjects: LCSH: Vegetarian cooking. | Vegan cooking. |
Food waste—Prevention. | LCGFT: Cookbooks.
Classification: LCC TX837.B567 2021 (print) | LCC TX837 (ebook) |
DDC 641.5/636—dc23
LC record available at https://lccn.loc.gov/2020025732
LC ebook record available at https://lccn.loc.gov/2020025733

p.   cm.

Printed in China
1 3 5 7 9 10 8 6 4 2

Book design by Ashley Tucker

For my daughters,
Mary Katherine and Charlotte

CONTENTS

1

Three, Two, One, Zero: Getting Started

American consumers generate, on average, 4½ pounds of trash per person every day. Much of this waste consists of materials we used briefly, like food packaging, or materials we didn't use at all, like food.

The way we consume is linear: We take raw materials to make products to dispose of them after their (usually short) life, which generates approximately 268 million tons of waste a year. A little over half of that waste ends up in landfills. As the waste decomposes, it belches methane gas into the atmosphere, a greenhouse gas 84 times more potent than carbon dioxide over a twenty-year period and excretes toxic leachate into the ground, which contaminates our groundwater.

Some of this waste escapes collection altogether and pollutes our natural environment. Every minute, the equivalent of one garbage truck full of plastic enters our oceans. On our current trajectory, the oceans will contain an estimated one ton of plastic for every three tons of fish by 2025, and by 2050, *more* plastic than fish. And it's not just the ocean: Tiny plastic particles from packaging, plastic mulch, and sewage sludge[1] contaminate the soil, as well, which threatens plants, animals, and humans alike.

We have polluted the planet with indestructible plastic to such a degree that plastic may serve as a fossil marker in our strata to indicate a new era—the way dinosaurs indicate the Mesozoic one—until Big Oil digs the last of those reptiles up to produce more Coke bottles.[2] Houston—and Los Angeles, and New York, and Chicago, and Toronto, and Phoenix, and Philadelphia, and San Francisco, and all the Springfields all over the place and Everytown everywhere—we have a problem.

Can't We Simply Recycle All the Plastic?

In the United States, our abysmal 9 percent recycling rate remained steady between 2012 and 2017, even as China imported a total of 700,000 tons of our plastic waste

1 Sewage sludge contains microplastics that have shed from synthetic clothing when washed in the washing machine.
2 Plastic is derived from oil.

between 2010 and 2016. In 2018, the year of reckoning arrived: China announced it would no longer serve as the West's dumping ground for our tossed plastic. By 2030, the world will need to bury, burn, or recycle an estimated 111 million metric tons of plastic. We can't possibly recycle our way out of this mess.

Even if we could improve our infrastructure and recycle 100 percent of our plastic, the Plastic Pollution Coalition reports that "recycling . . . plastic is generally not [a complete cycle] . . . The best we can hope for is that our plastic water bottles and mayonnaise jars will be turned into other products (downcycled), such as doormats, textiles, plastic lumber, etc. These products will still end up in a landfill." Of course, if we can recycle any of the plastic we produce, we should, but the real solution lies in reducing plastic at the source by manufacturing and consuming less of it.

Disposal aside, do we really want our food coming into contact with plastic? Exposure to the known endocrine disruptor bisphenol-A (BPA), a common additive in plastic food packaging, can lead to endometriosis, infertility, child loss, cancer, and genetic disorders. Because of public concern over BPA, some food producers have eliminated it from their food packaging. And while they can honestly plaster the claim "Now BPA-Free!" all over their packages, in a lot of cases they just use BPS or BPF—BPA replacements that raise similar health concerns.

Even seemingly innocuous compostable paper food packaging may contain "forever chemicals" like perfluoroalkyl substances (PFAS) that render materials grease- and water-proof. Because these substances never break down, they persist in the environment—forever. Studies have linked PFAS to adverse effects on metabolism, weight, fertility, fetal growth, and immune system response to infections.

What About Food Waste?

While addressing the plastic problem requires many approaches—the implementation of refill schemes, bans on single-use containers, eliminating unnecessary packaging, and so on—the problem of food waste has one simple solution: *We can eat the food.*

In developed countries, most food waste occurs at the consumer level; in our homes, we waste more food than grocery stores or restaurants, or any other stop along the supply chain. Every day, the average American wastes an astonishing near-one pound of food per person. When we squander food, we don't just waste the food itself; we misuse all the resources that went into producing it: the labor, the water, and the energy it took to grow and transport it, as well as the land, which we clear of carbon-sequestering trees to grow food that no one will eat.

Globally, food waste accounts for about 8 percent of greenhouse gas emissions.

(To put that into perspective, the aviation industry generates 2.5 percent.) Project Drawdown, a worldwide coalition of scientists and researchers, has compiled a list of the top 100 solutions to reduce global carbon emissions over a thirty-year period ending in 2050. Reducing food waste worldwide ranks at number three on their list, and is more effective than implementing rooftop solar power, offshore wind turbines, and electric vehicles *combined*.

Between food packaging and food waste, the kitchen presents the biggest opportunity for us to have an impact. But by how much can we reasonably reduce our waste?

What We Talk About When We Talk About Zero Waste

Is zero waste possible?

Before answering that question, let's start with the goal of zero waste, which is to prevent waste from entering landfills, incinerators, and the natural environment. Every piece of waste ever created began as a resource that we extracted from the earth. Zero waste is about conserving those resources.

As for the term itself, do not let the "zero" part intimidate you. As my daughter Charlotte once remarked, "The only true way to be zero-waste is to be dead." Even then, your family may serve bottled water at your funeral.

If you feel paralyzed by the zero (and would really rather not ponder your eventual demise), keep in mind that the term *zero waste* merely represents something to strive for, like an A+ in every class you take in college. But remember the saying, "Cs get degrees." You don't have to do zero waste perfectly to make an impact.

The size of that impact depends on how far you will—or can—go with the zero-waste program. You have likely seen images on social media of zero wasters posing with the trash they accumulated for a year—*or several years*—stored in a single mason jar. People tend to react to the trash jar in one of two ways:

1. They feel inspired to drastically reduce their trash to the same negligible amount—and they succeed!—or
2. Their eco-anxiety flares up, followed by feelings of paralysis, inadequacy, and guilt.

If you fall into the eco-anxiety category, or you do attempt to reduce your trash to one mason jar per year and simply cannot, do not beat yourself up. While I do believe it's possible for many people to reduce their yearly trash to an amount minuscule enough to fit into a mason jar, only a small number of people will. As you'll see, that's okay!

I'm going to think big about book sales—10,000 copies sold in the first week—and small about how many people will reach absolute zero waste. Let's say 100 readers—or 1 percent—reduced their waste to essentially zero. In a year, how much collective waste would those readers keep from entering the environment? Let's crunch the numbers:

100 people × 4.5 pounds reduced/day × 365 days = **164,250 pounds/year**

That's a lot of trash!

Now let's say that of those same 10,000 readers, 25 percent of them reduced their waste by 25 percent. How much total trash would that save us?

4.5 pounds × .25 = **1.125 pounds per day**
2,500 people × 1.125 pounds reduced/day × 365 days = **1,026,562.50 pounds/year**

Over a million pounds of trash! That's amazing. Now what if all 10,000 readers reduced their waste by just 10 percent for a year? Doesn't sound that impressive, does it? Well, let's see:

4.5 pounds × .10 = **.45 pounds per day**
10,000 people × .45 pounds reduced/day × 365 days = **1,642,500 pounds/year**

At 1,642,500 pounds, everyone doing a little bit makes the biggest impact of all three of these scenarios, as the graph that follows illustrates.

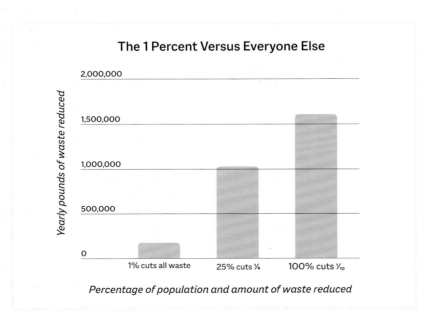

The 1 Percent Versus Everyone Else

Yearly pounds of waste reduced

2,000,000

1,500,000

1,000,000

500,000

0

1% cuts all waste   25% cuts ¼   100% cuts ¹⁄₁₀

Percentage of population and amount of waste reduced

Zero waste isn't an all-or-nothing proposition. Unlike pregnancy—you either are or you aren't—you can live a little bit zero waste. Some of the changes necessary to reach that 10 percent goal, which just about everyone can do, won't hurt one bit. And after you hit 10 percent, you likely won't stop there. You'll keep going because you reap so many rewards from this lifestyle.

What's in It for You

I started on this zero-waste journey in 2011 after reading about the devastating effects plastic pollution has on our oceans and their inhabitants. I wanted to cut plastic immediately (weaning actually took several months). I had no idea there would be so many personal benefits to kicking the plastic, much less life-changing ones.

My biggest surprise came when, after a couple of years into this lifestyle, I realized I hadn't felt so healthy in, well, a couple of years. I attribute this to my improved diet. When I eliminated the waste, I eliminated packaged, highly processed food. I never ate piles of the stuff, but now I eat none. Processed foods not only lack fiber and nutrients, they also throw our guts off balance; and as the research continues to reveal, our guts control every aspect of our health, from our immunity to our weight, to our mood, to food cravings and more. When I stopped buying packaged food, I started preparing more fermented food. How else would I get my sour cream? Fermented foods benefit gut health. These fermented foods—sourdough bread, kimchi, sauerkraut, dosas, hot sauce—also happen to taste delicious.

And even though I haven't dropped out of society to go live in a cabin by the pond, I'm more self-reliant now. I don't depend on corporations to fulfill my every need and desire because, despite Big Food's best efforts to keep us helpless in the kitchen, I don't need packaged frozen dinners or shelf-stable snacks to feed myself. Besides improving my cooking chops, I've brushed up on other skills that our grandparents and great-grandparents possessed, like sewing, mending, and DIY. If my grandmothers were alive today, they'd ask why on earth anyone would invite me onto a stage to show an audience how to make broth from food scraps or cloth produce bags from fabric scraps. "But that's just *normal*," they'd say.

Reducing my waste has also made me much happier. Every aspect of modern life in North America involves waste—from how we shop to what we eat, to how we dress, to how we travel. To reduce my waste, I had to examine every aspect of my life, make decisions more intentionally, slow down, and live more simply. It's made my life more fulfilling than mindless consuming ever did.

And if health, better-tasting food, increased independence, and happiness don't get you on board, perhaps money will. If for no other reason, reduce your waste to save cold, hard cash. Don't do it for the oceans. Don't do it to conserve resources so others may have a share of them. Don't do it for future generations. Be completely selfish about it. Your motives are your own business.

I'm Sold–But Where Do I Start?

Start where you are. But first, figure out where you are.

When we first went plastic free, my daughter Mary Kat participated in Beth Terry's plastic challenge (www.myplasticfreelife.com). This helped us realize what kind of plastic we had been throwing away or recycling. The vast majority of it came from the kitchen in the form of food packaging. I bet you'll discover the same thing.

You don't know how to address an issue if you don't measure it. Think of your finances. To get a handle on how you spend your money, you would examine your expenses. ("I spend *how much* on to-go coffee?!") Here, you'll examine how much trash you accumulate. ("I toss out *how many* to-go coffee cups?!")

To measure your waste, audit the trash you generate—those to-go coffee cups and lids, Tetra Paks, plastic produce bags, soda bottles, straws, and so on. Include recyclable plastic. You may want to conduct your audit for a few weeks.

You can jot down a list of the trash as you go through it or save it so at the end of the week you can take a picture of it on your phone. This audit will give you an idea of (1) how much trash you throw out and (2) which products you'll want to avoid or replace first. For example, if you find lots of snack wrappers, take a look at the snack recipes in this book (page 233) as a place to start.

How are we ever going to do this?

Back in the spring of 2011, after deciding we would give plastic-free living a try, Mary Kat and I took our first trip to the nearby chain supermarket, where we used to do lots of our shopping. We wheeled our cart around the store, frustrated by what we saw. Plastic was everywhere: suffocating the cauliflower and cucumbers in the produce section and lining the paper milk cartons in dairy. Even the pasta boxes had little plastic windows so shoppers could see what spaghetti looks like.

Finally, in the bathroom tissue aisle, I literally threw my hands up in the air. Surrounded by a sea of shrink-wrapped white rolls in every type and quantity— single-ply, double-ply, extra-soft, quilted, recycled, jumbo, 4 rolls, 8 rolls, 16 rolls, 32 rolls, I turned to Mary Kat and said, "How are we ever going to do this?"

But sure enough, step-by-step, swap-by-swap, we implemented the necessary changes to eliminate the plastic waste. Since that day in the bathroom tissue aisle, I've gone on to tackle the challenges and develop the recipes and address the dilemmas of a zero-waste life. With this book, you'll skip a big section of the learning curve on your own zero-waste journey.

And something magical happens along the way. At speaking engagements and meet-ups, in workshops and classes, interacting with my audience online and chatting with friends, family, and coworkers in person, I've witnessed the light bulbs go off—*I could do that!* people realize—as I describe a swap as simple to implement as shopping with a cloth produce bag. Others around you will notice what you're doing, and you'll inspire some of them to implement a change—or two or three or four—of their own. The more of us who are on board, the farther the ripples will spread out and the faster change happens.

2

Cooking Like Grandma

Our grandmothers and great-grandmothers were zero waste before zero waste was cool. They ran their kitchens efficiently, they used everything, and they wasted nothing. Although cooking the zero-waste way today bestows rebel status, several generations ago you would have just been, well, normal. Maybe boring. Now you write books.

In addition to adopting these new (old) methods, taking on Julia Child's what-the-hell, fearless attitude will help you adjust to this system of cooking—and it is a system. Don't be afraid to try new things and fail. Failure is merely one step closer to success. A lot of the good stuff happens out on that limb that may or may not hold the weight of your Dutch oven.

Freestyle Cooking

Here's a secret: You already have all the ingredients you need to make a meal.

Rather than allowing your cravings to dictate what you'll make, let the food you have on hand in your pantry, refrigerator, and freezer serve as the basis for your next dish. This method will eliminate food waste in the home.

Yes, eliminate.

This idea that we can let our pantry dictate dinner runs contrary to how most of us learned to shop and cook. Typically, we look up an appetizing recipe, jot down a shopping list, buy the ingredients, cook the dish and, after eating, store the leftover dish—and all the little bits of ingredients left over from cooking it—in the refrigerator, possibly to eat later but often not.

Relinquishing some control of our menus over to our kitchen inventories makes us not only more resourceful but also more creative, as parameters tend to do. And that makes cooking more fun.

When taking your kitchen inventory, keep in mind that food manufacturers stamp best-before dates, sell-by dates, and use-by dates on their products to indicate the peak of freshness. Your food does not turn deadly at the stroke of midnight on its best-before date. If a tub of yogurt past this date looks good, smells good, and tastes good, then you're good. (And besides, some products with best-before dates don't actually spoil because they're packed with preservatives.)

Learn how to cook without a recipe

I advocate that you learn to cook without a recipe, which may sound contradictory, considering that I've written a cookbook, but recipes are guidelines you can adapt.

This cookbook includes many customizable recipes, such as Granny's Pot Pie (page 220), Eat-All-Your-Vegetables Pancakes (page 172), Customizable Stir-Fry (page 181), Use-All-the-Vegetables Frittata (page 207), Ricotta and Ratatouille Galette (page 212), and more. I've also included ideas in many of the recipes for using up the scraps and leftovers that the recipes render.

Cook without strictly following recipes and you'll be able to cook whatever you find in your pantry. You have no moral obligation to strictly follow all the steps in my recipes, such as charring poblanos or blanching and peeling tomatoes, or toasting nuts before adding them to a recipe. While these steps improve a dish, you may prefer to skip them. You won't hurt my feelings!

If you don't know where to start with a freestyle dish, make soup. I usually make a weekly vat of it before I buy more food, using the following formula:

1. Heat 2 tablespoons of fat over medium heat.

2. Sauté 1 chopped onion until soft, about 5 minutes. Add spices, such as dried oregano or cumin or coriander, and stir for 1 minute.

3. Add random chopped vegetables—that ½ bell pepper, those 3 mushrooms, and 2 cabbage leaves hanging around. Stir for 2 minutes to evenly coat them with the oil and spices.

4. Chop up an apple and throw it in. Add that ¼ cup of mystery grains you discovered in the pantry and the 3 tablespoons of cooked rice in the refrigerator. Have some cheese rinds? First of all, congratulations for saving those. You're really getting the hang of this. Into the soup they go. Have leftover beans or other protein? Stir them in. Pour in enough broth or water to just barely cover everything.

5. Cook the soup until the vegetables and grains are tender. Add salt and lemon juice (or vinegar) and taste. Chop up some excess herbs and stir in at the end.

Before serving, swirl in a spoonful of crème fraîche or yogurt and garnish the soup with croutons you made from stale bread cubes that you toasted in the oven after tossing them in olive oil.

Do this and you've not only made a delicious, satisfying meal but have also prevented a pile of waste. Made too much rescue soup? Freeze some for several days or weeks, and enjoy it for lunch or dinner on a busy day.

Occasionally a dish won't turn out—as also can happen when strictly following a recipe—but generally, you'll cook delicious food this way while discovering flavors and combinations you may not have thought of otherwise.

Do remember to taste along the way as you create your use-it-up, non-recipe recipes. As you become more confident in the kitchen, you'll feel more comfortable adding a little bit of this herb or that vegetable.

Think ahead to the next recipe and use everything all the time

Slowing down and living in the present result in less waste because you live less of a go-go-go lifestyle, buy less on the fly, and make conscious decisions rather than mechanical ones. But when talking food waste, always think about the future.

As you chop and mince and stir, contemplate the next incarnation of the bits left over from prepping, or the leftover dish itself. If you make nut milk (see page 112), for example, you may decide to use some of the leftover pulp in granola (see page 158) the next day and some in the topping of the Any-Fruit Crunchy Crumble (page 268) the day after that. Hang on to the peels and cores from the apples you chose for your crumble to make Apple Scrap Vinegar (page 101). Use the vinegar to later make the As You Like It Honey Mustard (page 129). Add some mustard to the salad dressing for the One-Bean, One-Vegetable, One-Grain Salad (page 206). If you notice SCOBYs (symbiotic cultures of bacteria and yeast) growing in your scrap vinegar, use those to make Lemon Zesty Kombucha (page 255) and on and on and on.

Soaking or fermenting or proofing something on your kitchen counter nearly constantly will save time. By always having at least a couple of ingredients prepped and ready to go, you won't need to start a new dish every night from scratch. Who has time for that?

And when you have the oven on, make the most of it. Melt the coconut oil you'll need to make the dough for Sourdough Crackers with Everything-Bagel Seasoning (page 235) or bake Anything Goes Granola (page 158) along with the black-eyed pea and mushroom burgers (page 199). Or bake the soft burger buns (page 96) at the same time as you roast some vegetables (see page 176). But only multitask as much as you can handle.

It's meal-planning lite; you don't need to plan for every little morsel of food you'll eat over the next week and enter it into a complicated spreadsheet (unless you want to!). Using what you find in your pantry in step one, drawing on your repertoire of adaptable recipes in step two, and getting creative with leftover ingredients and meals in step three, you plan your next two or three meals. Like all things zero waste, a bit of planning stops waste before it happens, like preventive medicine. As you plan some of your meals, expect the unexpected from time to time. Impromptu work lunches or last-minute dinner invitations will throw off your plans, and that's okay.

Preserve Food in the Freezer

Yes, the freezer compartment of your refrigerator consumes energy, but most people living indoors have a freezer. The fossil fuel that runs it doesn't care if you fill your freezer or not, so you may as well fill it. Cook and freeze large amounts of food to enjoy later, preserve seasonal foods like summer berries, and prevent food waste by squirreling away food that you won't eat immediately.

Freezing without plastic

When I post pictures of my jar-filled freezer on social media, I get lots of questions about it, usually along the following lines:

Is it safe to freeze food in glass? (Yes.)

Do you use special glass for the freezer? (No, I use a variety of everyday jars—recycled jars, mason jars, big jars, small jars.)

Don't your glass containers break? (Only that one time.)

I have had little trouble freezing food in glass. I do however take precautions:

- **Always leave headspace in jars.** When liquid freezes, it expands. If you don't leave space for this expansion, your glass jar can break.

- **Choose wide-mouth jars without necks or shoulders.** Straight, flush sides work best for freezing. I have broken only one glass container in the freezer—it's one of those things you rarely repeat. I filled a narrow-neck milk bottle with liquid. Even though I had left headspace, when the liquid froze, it expanded and snapped the narrow neck cleanly off the (very nice) bottle. Oops.

- **Don't overstuff your freezer with jars stacked all over the place willy-nilly.** When you open your freezer door, jars might fall out onto the floor and land on your toes, or break.

- **Cool the food at room temperature.** Don't put jars full of hot food into the freezer. I have noticed that when I allow the food to cool at room temperature and then chill it overnight in the refrigerator before freezing it, very few ice crystals form on top of the food.

- **Thaw in the refrigerator.** The night before you need it, transfer your jar of frozen food to the refrigerator to thaw or at least thaw enough so that you can remove the food from the jar to heat it or cook with it. Reducing your waste does mean you need to plan ahead, but not that much.

People also ask me about freezer burn. Freezer burn occurs when water molecules in your food escape in search of colder parts of the freezer. The food, while safe to eat, takes on an unappealing texture, with frozen water molecules on its surface. Even though I don't use plastic, I don't have many problems with freezer burn. Food doesn't last indefinitely in the freezer, however. For optimal taste and texture, eat most foods within six months. Eat bread within a week or two.

Just some of what I freeze

- **Beans.** I cook beans in my pressure cooker and freeze extra beans in jars. I usually freeze them in their broth. I also freeze broth from cooked beans to use later in various dishes calling for vegetable broth.

- **Bread.** When I bake sourdough bread, I usually freeze a whole loaf in a homemade cloth produce bag. I find that slices get freezer burn quickly. I also don't freeze bread for very long—a couple of weeks maximum.

- **Cookies.** I don't make cookies very often because I have little willpower around sweets. But when I do bake them, I freeze some.

- **Crackers.** My sourdough crackers freeze very well! They taste so delicious, though, they never stay in the freezer long (see page 235).

- **Eggs.** Crack them into a jar, whisk them, and freeze them. Egg whites also freeze well.

- **Fruit.** I don't buy frozen fruit because it's always packaged in plastic bags. Instead, I freeze fruit near the end of the season: strawberries, cherries, peach slices, and grapes. I wash them, slice them or pit them, spread them out on a cookie sheet in a single layer, and put that in the freezer. Once the fruit has frozen, I transfer it to glass jars. By freezing this way, I end up with frozen loose berries rather than a frozen fruit blob I can't pry apart.

- **Fruit peels and cores.** If you don't eat many apples but want to make the Apple Scrap Vinegar (page 101), freeze the scraps until you have accumulated enough of them to make vinegar. The microbes necessary for the fermentation survive in the freezer and take a little nap. (See page 40.)

- **Lemon zest.** Yes, you can freeze this! Use a small jar.

- **Pizza sauce.** Having this on hand speeds up pizza production. See the recipe on page 227.

- **Roasted tomatoes.** In the summer, I roast and freeze at least a couple crates of Early Girl tomatoes and use these in place of canned tomatoes. See page 121 for the instructions.

- **Soup.** I love to make a vat of soup and freeze some of it in jars for future quick lunches and dinner.

Short-Term Food Storage

Read aloud in a Brad Pitt drawl: "The first rule of food waste is: You do not buy too much food. The second rule of food waste is: you do not buy too much food." The next rule is to store food properly.

Fresh fruit and vegetables go to waste more than other foods. In an ideal world—one in which you have time to shop a few times a week at a local farmers' market that runs daily—you'd buy what you need and eat it at its peak of freshness, flavor, and nutrition. Or you would stroll outside into your yard and pluck what you need from your lush, prolific, year-round garden. For most of us, these scenarios are neither possible nor practical. But if we store our produce with care, less of it will spoil before we can eat it.

Kitchen Chemistry: Ethylene Gas

Ethylene, a small hydrocarbon gas, causes fruit to ripen. It softens it and changes its texture and flavor. Many types of fruit and some vegetables produce this hormone naturally. Some Big Food producers use it unnaturally to ripen fruit they pick early, such as tomatoes. By picking unripe, hard, green tomatoes and gassing them to turn them red, producers can ship the tomatoes long distances without damaging them. They taste terrible but survive long hauls and live up to the cosmetic standards of the day.

Some types of ethylene-sensitive produce over-ripen and spoil when exposed to ethylene. So it's best to keep ethylene-producing foods away from ethylene-sensitive foods.

Ethylene producers include

- Apples
- Apricots
- Avocados
- Bananas
- Cantaloupe
- Peaches
- Pears
- Plums
- Tomatoes

Ethylene-sensitive foods include

- Apples
- Asparagus
- Broccoli
- Brussels sprouts
- Carrots
- Cauliflower
- Cucumbers
- Eggplants
- Green beans
- Kale
- Lemons
- Lettuce
- Onions
- Parsley
- Peas
- Summer squash
- Sweet potatoes
- Watermelon

Some types of produce, such as apples, can dish it out but can't take it—they both produce ethylene and are sensitive to it. Confused? When in doubt, follow this basic rule: Separate fruit and vegetables and keep bananas away from everything. However, if you do want that hard avocado to ripen faster, place it in a bowl of ripening fruit.

Where to Store Produce for Optimal Freshness

If you will eat what you buy within one to three days, most of your produce will keep well on the kitchen counter, away from direct sunlight. But the truth is most of us can't shop every couple of days.

Store it outside the refrigerator

Refrigerator temperatures—generally around the mid-30s Fahrenheit range—damage the flavor and texture of many types of produce. Never store tomatoes in the refrigerator unless you enjoy a mealy texture bereft of flavor. Keep them at room temperature (ideally, not too warm a room), along with avocados, bananas, melons, pumpkins, potatoes (including sweet potatoes), and winter squash. Onions and shallots also keep better without refrigeration but away from potatoes, as the two react and can speed up each other's demise.

Store it inside the refrigerator

After harvest, vegetables continue to breathe, consuming oxygen and emitting carbon dioxide and water. Vegetables that respirate at a higher rate keep better in the refrigerator crisper, where food retains more moisture than in the open space of the main refrigerator compartment, which can draw moisture out of produce. Vegetables with higher respiration rates include artichokes, asparagus, broccoli, Brussels sprouts, scallions, mushrooms, and sweet corn.

Store your breathing vegetables in cloth produce bags so they can continue to breathe. Larger vegetables like cabbage and cauliflower don't require a produce bag to transport home and can go naked into the crisper.

Store it in a jar of water

Some vegetables keep for a long time stored in a jar of water at room temperature. These include asparagus, basil, and celery.

Composting

Ideally, all of us would eat all the food we buy, but waste happens. You get sick and can't eat what you bought, your kids eat dinner at their friends' houses instead of at home, or you simply overbuy. When you can't eat it, ferment it, freeze it, or feed it to your chickens (because you have no chickens) and it spoils, compost it. Spoiled food belongs in a compost, not a landfill.

Compacted in a landfill, food lacks exposure to oxygen and so breaks down anaerobically, releasing methane gas into the atmosphere, which we know is eighty-four times more potent than carbon dioxide over a twenty-year period.

On the other hand, take that same food waste, break it down into compost, and it can reduce greenhouse gas emissions. When farmers and gardeners apply that compost to the soil, it actually enhances the soil's ability to draw carbon dioxide out of the atmosphere.

If you have a patch of dirt in your yard, you can start composting today. Collect your food scraps—fruit and vegetable peels, scraps of food your kids didn't finish at lunch, moldy produce, but nothing oily—in a large container and toss them on the ground at the end of the day. Cover them with brown matter (dry leaves, for example). Tomorrow, repeat. Or add scraps every few days. Keep the pile about as damp as a squeezed sponge. Or build or buy a bin.

Live in a cold climate? My sister composts year-round in the Great White North. She tosses her scraps on her compost heap outside. They freeze. They thaw. They rot.

If you live in an apartment and have no yard, consider vermicompost (composting with worms). You'll keep a bin of red worms in a convenient location and feed them various food scraps. They'll convert those food scraps to earthy-smelling, nutrient-rich material that you can add to houseplants or give to gardening friends.

Your city may also provide either curbside pickup of food waste or drop-off sites. Contact your city's waste management department to inquire if it offers this service.

Cleaning

Clean as you go! The managers at the fast-food restaurant I worked in as a teenager drilled this into us, and it has always stuck with me. Cleaning as you go helps keep your kitchen running smoothly and efficiently.

To wash dishes, look for solid dishwashing soap blocks or dishwashing liquid in bulk. Baking soda or vinegar or both works wonders for cleaning. I use my homemade Apple Scrap Vinegar (page 101) or kombucha (page 255) I've let ferment to the point of strong vinegar to clean with rags I cut from old T-shirts. Reusable unpaper towels also work well.

3

Changing the Culture: Fermentation

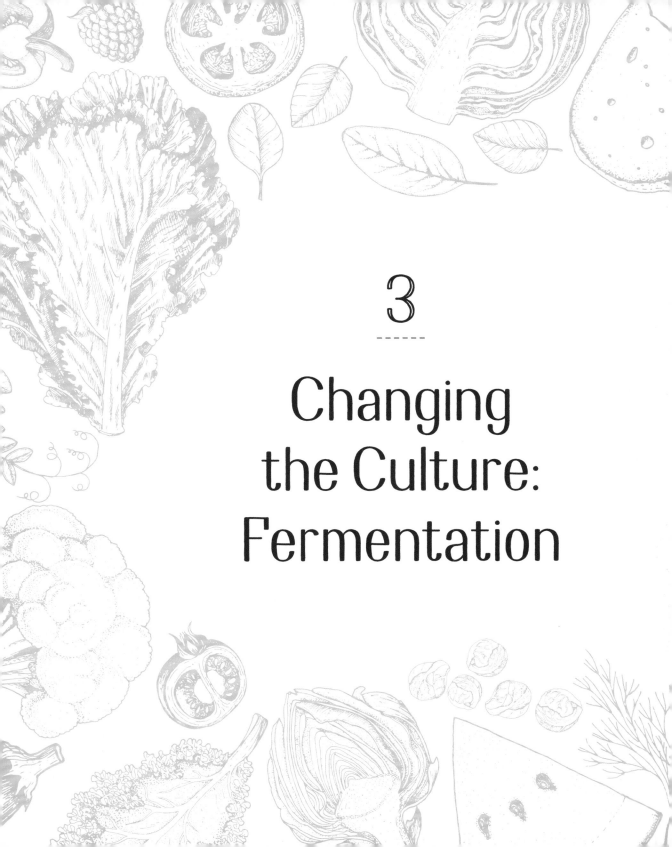

Humans have fermented food for thousands of years and across cultures. This method of food preparation harnesses the beneficial bacteria and yeast present in foods, in the air, and on our hands to transform that food into something greater—and tastier—than the sum of its parts.

Many people who fall down the rabbit hole of low-waste living will eventually stumble upon the magic of fermentation. You may start with vinegar, and once you realize how tasty and low-cost it is, want to branch out into sourdough bread, "pickled" vegetables, yogurt, and ginger beer.

In this book, you'll find recipes for fermented grains, produce, legumes, dairy, and beverages. While each group may produce different types of intensely flavored fermented foods, they all begin with a similar method: fill a jar with food, cover it, and wait. For advanced recipes, stir daily. Even though the "and wait" step runs counter to the consumer culture so many of us grew up in, too much convenience has created an ecological crisis. "And wait" must play a role in addressing it.

The Benefits of Fermentation

It's no wonder fermentation has been undergoing a renaissance over the past several years when you consider how much we benefit from this traditional method of food preparation, especially when we do it at home. Let's count the ways.

Food preservation, not food waste

Fermentation extends the shelf life of foods and offers a way to preserve food in our homes before it can become waste. Take milk, for example. Warm up fresh milk, add a few spoonfuls of cultured yogurt to it, let it rest overnight in a warm spot, and by morning, the bacteria present in the small amount of yogurt you added will have transformed your milk into a fresh batch of yogurt, which keeps for many weeks longer than the original milk would have.

Delicious results

The most cherished and often most expensive foods—sourdough bread, kimchi, kombucha, pickles, sour cream, cheese, beer, wine, vinegar, chocolate, coffee, tea, and so on—rely on the process of fermentation, which renders distinctive, complex, and intense flavors. If you'd like to adopt a more plant-rich diet for environmental or health reasons—or both—but worry your meals will taste bland unless umami-rich meat and fish take center plate, then ferment yourself a batch of Pick-Your-Peppers Hot Sauce (page 91), Simple Spicy Kimchi (page 187), or Preserved Lemons (page 95) to serve on the side of any vegetable-forward dish. These condiments all add dynamic flavor to any meal. Crave a little snack? Tangy sourdough crackers taste cheesy but contain no cheese.

Less anxiety, healthier bodies

Going plastic free in 2011 forced me to clean up my diet. In addition to cutting out all highly processed foods (almost all of which come in a plastic package) and starting to eat more fiber-rich whole foods—vegetables, fruit, legumes, and whole grains—I also began making and eating more fermented foods. As a result, I rarely get sick now.

Not only am I physically healthier but I also feel less anxious. (I am a naturally anxious person from a long line of naturally anxious people.) I could chalk up my reduced anxiety to maturity, the wisdom that comes with age, and an intrinsic, rare insight into the human condition. But really, I think it's the yogurt. Many recent studies have provided compelling evidence that probiotics help alleviate symptoms of anxiety.

But if my anecdotal evidence does not convince you to start a batch of dilly beans, how's this?

- Like an external stomach, fermentation predigests food, making digestion easier for our bodies.

- Fermentation reduces levels of antinutrients in food. Phytates, present in grains, nuts, seeds, beans, and lentils, bind to minerals, making those minerals unavailable for absorption. Fermentation breaks these bonds to make the nutrients available.

Why Fermentation Is So Safe

Online and in person, people constantly tell me that their fear of accidentally poisoning and killing their entire family with botulism-laced vegetables has prevented them from fermenting food in their home kitchens. In reality, fermentation is safer than many other forms of food preparation.

Anaerobic lactic-acid bacteria naturally occur on all plants. When you cut off oxygen to these bacteria by submerging, for example, chopped cabbage in liquid, the bacteria eat the sugars in the cabbage, reproduce, and produce lactic acid. The lactic acid not only transforms the cabbage into tangy sauerkraut but also inhibits the growth of bad bacteria. Even *C. botulinum*, the spores that cause botulism, cannot survive in a lactic-acid fermentation. They don't grow below a pH of 4.6 (acidic sauerkraut ferments below this pH level).

Microbiologist Fred Breidt, a USDA researcher who specializes in the study of fermented foods, states, "With fermented products there is no safety concern. I can flat-out say that. The reason is the lactic acid bacteria that carry out the fermentation are the world's best killers of other bacteria." Raw vegetables, he points out, can pose a greater health risk than fermented vegetables if contaminated with E. coli from the farm on which they grew.

As you would with any type of food preparation, follow basic food safety guidelines when fermenting food. Before starting, wash your hands and clean cutting surfaces and tools with hot, soapy water. Other than that, you shouldn't worry.

- Fermentation naturally fortifies food. Certain strains of lactic acid bacteria (LAB) increase the levels of the B vitamins riboflavin, folate, and niacin in yogurt. The long fermentation of sourdough preserves significantly more of the thiamin and riboflavin present in the grains than a short fermentation. (B vitamins are important to cellular health and function. In addition, riboflavin, niacin, and thiamine help convert food to energy. Folate helps form DNA and RNA.)

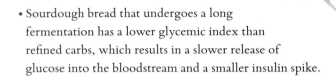

- Sourdough bread that undergoes a long fermentation has a lower glycemic index than refined carbs, which results in a slower release of glucose into the bloodstream and a smaller insulin spike.

- The long fermentation of sourdough bread breaks down gluten more than commercial yeast does, which may benefit those with gluten intolerance.

- Fermented fruits and vegetables can provide probiotics, which are beneficial bacteria.

Minimal energy consumption and effort

Fermented foods take very little—if any—energy to prepare. The energy required to transform a jar of cabbage into sauerkraut comes from the bacteria within the jar, not from an outside source, such as fracked gas or "clean coal," whatever that might be. Once "cooked," that sauerkraut can keep for months at room temperature (unless the room is very warm) without the need for refrigeration. As we make the necessary transition away from fossil fuels, fermented foods can play a role in how we prepare our food.

Plus, fermented foods are easy to prepare, requiring only the most basic cooking skills. If you can cut a cabbage with a knife, you can make sauerkraut. If you can brew tea, you can make kombucha. Almost every time I've fermented something new, I've thought to myself, "Is that all there is to it? How did I not already know how to do this?"

Economical

You can spend a lot of money on special equipment to ferment food, but you don't need to. See pages 58 to 60 for tools you'll need. Even if you do buy some fancy tools, you'll recoup your money in no time with what you'll save making your own fermented foods.

A small tub of store-bought crème fraîche costs about $7. I can make the same amount with pasture-raised, organic cream for half the price. A bottle of store-bought kombucha costs between $4 to $5. I can make a 16-ounce bottle of my homemade version, using the best organic loose-leaf tea I can find, for 50 cents maximum. A small jar of preserved lemons will set you back about $8. The lemon tree in my yard provides free lemons, so my preserved lemons cost basically nothing to make.

Homemade fermented foods cost less than store bought and a fraction of what probiotic supplements do. As Justin and Erica Sonnenburg, pioneering researchers into the crucial role our microbiota plays in our health, state in their book, *The Good Gut*, that because we don't know how a specific probiotic supplement will affect us, we're more likely to benefit from eating fermented foods because they contain a much wider range of microbes.

For the price of one bottle of probiotic pills I can ferment a six-month supply of sauerkraut or many jars of yogurt. And they taste better.

Fermentation is an act of defiance

For me, a jar of homemade sauerkraut isn't just a tasty, healthy snack. It's also an act of defiance against our broken food system. Making our own food transforms us from passive consumers to active makers. It reduces our dependence on Big Food to feed us.

I'm not claiming that fermentation will save the world. But preparing food this way does put us more in tune with the natural world—the food is alive, after all—and that might lead us to better preserve and protect that world.

Troubleshooting

Although very safe (see box on page 35), fermentations can and do sometimes go awry.

Sourdough dense and doesn't rise

Keep in mind that baking with sourdough requires practice. Unlike baking with baker's yeast, which always works, the temperature and humidity of your kitchen, the type of flour you use, and even the bacteria on your hands will affect your sourdough. Be patient and take lots of notes. If you keep baking bricks, you could be letting the bulk fermentation go too long. Many beginning bakers do this, hoping to get a better rise in their bread. But eventually the dough will begin to break down and collapse into a puddle, reverting back to a starter.

Kahm yeast

You diligently saved all the scraps, peels, and cores from your homemade apple crumble (see page 268) and put them in a jar with water and a bit of sugar to brew your first batch of scrap vinegar. All goes well for a couple of weeks—bubbles appear, the fruity aroma turns alcoholic, then vinegary. You make big plans for this inaugural batch. Then one morning, you peer into the jar only to discover that a beige, dryish film has developed on top of the liquid. Your heart sinks.

Don't toss out that ferment! Most likely you have encountered your first—and likely not last—invasion of kahm yeast. This harmless, merely annoying yeast often forms on the surface of sweeter ferments, such as fruit or beets, after the microbes have eaten most of the sugars and cannot produce the acids necessary to ferment successfully. Simply scrape off as much kahm yeast as possible with a clean spoon. You likely won't get it all. If it reappears, scrape again. To prevent kahm yeast from forming in liquids such as your scrap vinegar, stir it several times a day to help prevent the microbe from taking up residence.

Moldy or mushy vegetables

Left to its own devices, kahm yeast can develop into dreaded, yet fairly rare, mold. In the event that mold strikes your fermenting veggies, you will recognize it. It will look like mold you've seen on bread—raised; furry; and, most commonly, white, green, or black in color. The top layer of vegetables may also turn brown and mushy when exposed to the air. Compost this layer and submerge the remaining vegetables better.

If white mold develops, scrape off as much as you can. If other colors appear—orange, pink, green, or black—remove and compost the entire layer of affected vegetables. To help prevent mold from forming on your next attempt—don't give up!—store your fermenting food in a room or section of a room that is neither too hot nor too cold. The Goldilocks temperature runs between 65°F and 70°F. Adding enough salt also inhibits the growth of unwanted bacteria. And always begin with clean hands, a clean work surface, and clean equipment.

Mold cannot develop in liquid, where it is cut off from the oxygen it requires to thrive. It can only develop on the surface of liquid or on rogue vegetables poking through the surface of liquid. People often send me pictures of their kombucha, mistaking the long brown strands of yeast that form below the surface for mold. These strands signify successful fermentation. As with fermenting vegetables, mold on the surface of kombucha or on the surface of its SCOBY looks like mold. Unfortunately, you can't salvage this. Certain highly toxic species of *Aspergillus* mold can develop on kombucha. (Other *Aspergillus* species are not toxic.) Pour your kombucha out and compost the SCOBYs. If you have created a SCOBY hotel, start over with a spare SCOBY (see page 257). To prevent mold from developing in your new batch, inoculate it with kombucha or apple cider vinegar with the live mother (see page 102), always add that kombucha or vinegar and the SCOBY *after* the tea has cooled, and keep your SCOBY at room temperature, where it will continue to produce the acid necessary to prevent mold.

If mold develops on the surface of your sourdough starter, remove it. If it appears more entrenched, you may want to start over. Use your judgment. If mold forms not on the starter itself but somewhere inside its house—the jar—remove a bit of the starter and feed it in a new, clean jar. Your sourdough starter may also begin to smell off— very vinegary, alcoholic, or even like dirty socks. A couple of feedings should remedy these strong odors and put your starter back on track. The first time mine smelled like acetone, I thought I had killed it, but it was hungry, not dead.

Shriveled SCOBY

If your SCOBY shrivels up or develops holes, it may simply dislike the sweetener you fed it. You need real sugar. Do not use stevia. If you want to experiment with sweeteners such as honey or maple syrup, or molasses, wait until you have extra SCOBYs to experiment with. Sugar works, and when you use it, you'll also learn how your kombucha (or your ginger bug, for that matter) should behave and look. Choose from table sugar, organic cane sugar, rapadura, coconut sugar, sucanat, or jaggery.

The amount of sugar you add to your kombucha and other fermented drinks may horrify you. But the bacteria and yeasts need the sugar to survive and thrive. They consume the bulk of it.

Overly vinegary kombucha

Once your kombucha has fermented, it will contain much less sugar. If you let it ferment long enough, it will contain very little sugar but will taste so vinegary you may not want to drink it (you will have good homemade vinegar on hand, however). Stop the fermentation sooner with your next batch. You can also combine the too-vinegary batch with the newer, too-sweet batch to balance out the sweet and sour flavors.

Inactivity

Especially when you attempt a new ferment, as you wait in anticipation for it to spring to life, it may seem as though it never will, when it suddenly does. Several factors can inhibit fermentation.

Temperature

Because a cold environment will slow down the process of fermentation, simply moving your jar to a warmer spot may solve the problem.

Chlorinated water

High levels of chlorine in tap water can prevent fermentation from taking place. The chlorine in our water supply kills both bad and good microbes—including the beneficial bacteria and yeasts necessary for fermentation. If your whole vegetables, kombucha, sourdough starter, or other fermented foods that call for water struggle to bubble to life and your tap water smells strongly of chlorine, you may have discovered the source of the problem. Fortunately, you can pretty easily remove chlorine from the water in a few ways.

For a low-tech, plan-ahead tactic, fill a wide-mouth jar or large bowl with water, cover it with a cloth to keep contaminants from falling in, and wait a day or two. The chlorine will evaporate from the wide surface area. When you need your water sooner, boil it for 20 minutes, uncovered. You must allow it to cool before you add it to the food you ferment, as heat will *also* kill the microbes in your fermented food. Some filters can also remove chlorine.

More and more municipalities have begun to treat the water supply with chloramine, a combination of chlorine and ammonia. Chloramine will not evaporate or boil off. A very good, not-inexpensive filter will remove chloramine, however.

Irradiation

Although I choose organic produce, both organic and non-organic will ferment. However, when fermenting ginger, choose organic ginger. Non-organic ginger may have undergone irradiation, a process that applies radiation briefly to food in order to eliminate microorganisms. Irradiation kills not only the bad microbes but also the good ones, and your ginger-based recipe may not ferment. Ginger—like all foods—cannot be labeled organic if it has been irradiated.

Missed feedings

Inactive starters such as sourdough and ginger bug may simply need food. To ensure you feed them regularly, keep track of feedings, at least initially. Although quite hardy, if you don't feed your starters, they can die. Write the dates of their last feedings on their jars with a china marker or mark the dates on a calendar. I line up my jars of kombucha SCOBYs on a shelf, ranging in order from most recently fed (far left) to least recently fed (far right).

4

What *Can't* a Jar Do? The Tools

To run your zero-waste kitchen, you'll need the proper tools. But make sure you're not bringing anything into your home that you don't need or won't use. To riff on Michael Pollan's maxim for eating, when equipping your kitchen—or when shopping in general—buy quality, not too much, mostly used.

Ideally, your kitchen tools will serve more than one purpose. You could buy a banana-shape tool that slices bananas into even slices; a special pliable plastic cone that peels garlic; and another tool that cuts, pits, and slices avocados. Or you could buy one chef's knife for all these tasks and more.

In this chapter, I assume you own basic gear such as mixing bowls, measuring cups and measuring spoons, baking sheets and baking dishes, wooden spoons, and so on. I list the zero-waste basics and some of the tools that you'll need to cook the recipes in this book.

Think before you buy, though. The best way to reduce your waste is to reduce your consumption. If you think you need something, wait a week or so before buying it. After a week, you may either have forgotten about it, decided you don't need it, or found a solution at home for free. For example, perhaps you thought you needed to buy plastic containers to store leftovers in but found a couple of large jars in the back of the cupboard to use instead. You've not only reduced your consumption, you now can see at a glance what you've stored in the jars, which will help you reduce food waste.

The Zero-Waste Chef's Tools

Jars

The three gadgets I use most in my kitchen are:

1. Jars
2. Jars
3. Jars

I had no idea when I went plastic free in 2011 that I would develop a jar obsession. I can't hoard enough jars, although I won't settle for just any jar I can get my hands on (a good rule to follow for just about everything in life). I covet jam jars the way some people covet shoes. If you haven't already, start collecting as many jars as seems rational—and then collect that same amount again.

Jar uses

Storing food

• **Keep your fresh produce fresh.** We know that basil, asparagus, and celery all keep well in a jar of water sitting on the counter.

• **See what's on hand.** If you store leftover chili in an opaque container, you may forget about it until you stumble upon its inedible remains a couple of months later. Store food in glass in your refrigerator, your freezer, and your cupboards, and you can see what's in there at a glance, which helps reduce food waste.

• **Freeze food.** I use glass jars for freezing all kinds of food. Stick with wide-mouth jars with flush sides. Rounded "shoulders" can break. Allow hot food to cool before putting it in the freezer. See more on page 24.

Prepping food

• Rolling out dough in a pinch
• Feeding and storing my sourdough starter, Eleanor
• Making vanilla extract

- Storing half an avocado in the refrigerator with some chopped onion to keep it fresh
- Straining yogurt to make Greek yogurt or labneh (yogurt cheese)
- Sprouting seeds
- Brewing kombucha
- Fermenting anything

Make your jar-filling life easier and get a wide-mouth funnel. It makes filling jars easy without slopping food all over the place. I've had my stainless steel wide-mouth funnel for at least twenty years. They last forever.

When you need more jars

You can spend a lot of money on beautiful, matching jars or you can start saving all the jars you buy food in and put these existing jars to use. Do this and when shopping, you may find yourself reading ingredient labels on jars only *after* you've examined the jar itself and have found the design worthy of joining your collection. When you've reached this point, your jar addiction has advanced beyond any known cure.

You'd also be amazed at the number of places you can find abandoned jars: the recycling bins where you live or work, and local restaurants, cafes, and bars. Finally, nurture your jar-crazed reputation and your friends, family, and neighbors will likely start saving their jars for you—until they catch the jar-hoarding bug.

De-labeling and de-smellifying jars

Unlike with brand-new empty jars you buy, the upcycled ones will require a bit of cleanup. Chalk this fact of zero-waste life up to TANSTAAFJ: there ain't no such thing as a free jar.

Most of these food jars have labels stuck to them. And often the biggest and best jars had once housed something pickled in them. In other words, the lids smell. Both problems have simple solutions.

1. Try to remove the label with water

If you are lucky, you can soak the jars in water for several hours and the labels will peel right off in one go. This technique often works with paper labels.

2. If water doesn't work, use oil

Or just start with oil and skip the water. Even after soaking in water, often some of the label or glue remains and oil will help dissolve that. If you have any oil that has gone rancid, save it for removing labels from jars and bottles.

Smear the label with oil and wait overnight. Peel off what you can. You may need to reapply more oil and repeat.

Adding baking soda to the oil makes a paste that sticks to the jars. If you have a tiny bit of peanut butter remaining in a peanut butter jar you want to de-label, smear that on the label and let it sit.

3. Remove sticky residue

A dough scraper or credit card work well to remove thick, sticky residue. After removing as much gunk as possible, scrub the rest off with a copper scrubber or baking soda.

4. Smelly lids

You can easily remove the pickle (or other) smell from a glass jar simply by washing it. Alas, this won't work for lids.

I have found that the best and easiest way to eliminate the smell in lids is to put them smelly side up outside in the sun for several hours on a bright day. I was amazed the first time I tried this. It works so well, consumes no energy—either from the grid or from you—and costs nothing.

Cook's Tools

One good knife. In his best-selling memoir *Kitchen Confidential*, Anthony Bourdain recommends buying one good chef's knife rather than a giant wooden block full of knives that you'll never use. I have a whole set of ridiculously expensive knives that an old boyfriend bought for me years ago that I don't need. I can only imagine what he felt so guilty about. I use my 7-inch chef's knife every day. I also use my paring knife and bread knife daily. But if you buy only one knife for now, start with the chef's knife.

Wooden cutting board. A 2019 study found that the average person may be eating a credit card's worth of microplastic each week, or about 5 grams. Most of the plastic we ingest comes from water and also from shellfish. But do you really want any more of your food coming into contact with plastic? Chop on wood. Knead on wood. Roll pastry on wood. Wood looks beautiful and it lasts.

Tapered wooden rolling pin. Any rolling pin will do the job, but I find a tapered one works best for evenly rolling out pastry, crackers, and doughs such as the Sourdough Sticky Buns (page 155). A pasta machine is very nice to have for making pasta, but you can also make pasta with a rolling pin (see page 209).

Baking stone. If you don't have this, use a cookie sheet to bake pizza on or a large cast-iron pan. If you do have this but don't have a Dutch oven for baking sourdough bread, use your baking stone.

Pizza peel. This makes sliding pizza onto the pizza stone and pulling it out easy. You can also serve the pizza on it.

Pizza wheel. A knife works also, but in addition to cutting pizza, a pizza wheel also makes quick work of cutting out homemade crackers.

Metal whisk. Use this for sifting dry ingredients, for whisking up a bechamel sauce, and for much more.

Sieve and a thin cloth. You'll use this combo often when straining vegetable broth, nut milks, tepache, and more. If you have a nut milk bag, you can use that instead.

Food mill. I use my food mill to remove the skins from tomatoes and to purée roasted vegetables, like pumpkin. If you don't have a food mill, you can use a food processor for some tasks.

Your senses and your brain. I did appreciate my digital thermometer during its short life. Today, after much practice, to make my yogurt, proof commercial yeast for dough, or gauge the temperature of water for my sourdough leaven, I am able to use my senses.

When making yogurt, I can tell from the appearance of bubbles just beginning to form around the edge of the pot that the milk has hit that desired, near-scalding-but-not-quite-scalding temperature. When I proof baker's yeast, I can sense from touching the water whether it has reached the correct temperature (around 110°F). This ability to sense "doneness" comes with practice, so you may want a thermometer when you start out; but after it breaks, if you have cooked regularly, you may not need it. Of course, never stick your finger into scalding-hot water!

Similarly, you do not need apps or a $6,000 smart refrigerator to alert you when your food will go bad. If you think that your leftover pot pie has turned, smell it and look at it. If it looks fine and passes the sniff test, it is probably fine.

Small Appliances

Many promising small appliances end up sitting in a cupboard, unused and taking up precious space. However, I do own several small appliances that slash my prep time and have thus earned their rightful place in my small kitchen.

Food processor. A food processor makes quick work of pastry. Use it also for making nut butters, pesto, batter, and more. For some recipes, you can use a blender instead, depending on the kind you have.

Spice grinder. Use this to make the topping for the Stovetop Popcorn with Nacho Cheese Seasoning (page 247), to grind up spices or superfine vanilla sugar, and more.

Blender. Use this for making nut milks, salsa for the huevos rancheros, the chili spice blend, and more. I found our basic blender on Craigslist for less than the cost of sales tax on a new fancy blender. I like that mine has a glass carafe. Hot food doesn't come into contact with plastic.

Waffle iron. You'll have trouble making waffles without one of these.

Pressure cooker. You can cook beans in a pot, a slow cooker, or a pressure cooker. I prefer a pressure cooker, since it cooks soaked beans in a fraction of the time they cook on the stovetop or in a slow cooker. In minutes, I can cook whole pie pumpkins or make vegetable broth in it. Bonus: Using a pressure cooker slashes your energy consumption.

Bread maker. This is your oven.

Cookware

If I could travel back in time, I would stop my younger self from accumulating all those nonstick pots and pans she cooked in for many years and buy her stainless steel, cast iron, and enameled cast-iron for her cookware instead. (I would also tell her to steer clear of that Antonio guy.)

Nonstick coatings expose consumers to those forever chemicals, PFAS, or perfluoroalkyl substances, which render pans slick enough to fry an egg on without adding fat—that demonized macronutrient banished from diets beginning in the late '70s. The misguided attempt to eliminate fat that our body needs increased our exposure to chemicals that it doesn't. Fat not only tastes good, but it also provides energy, enables the absorption of certain vitamins and minerals, supports cell growth, protects our organs, and more. If you prefer to cook on a nonstick surface, use cast iron repeatedly to build one up.

Whether you want to slowly replace your nonstick cookware or buy your very first pots and pans, by choosing a piece here and there, you'll assemble a smaller set that you'll both like and use. You'll probably also save money, especially if you can find some of your pieces secondhand.

Stainless steel

I use my stainless steel saucepans to cook rice, poach eggs, steam vegetables, pop popcorn, and more. A stockpot works well for broth, soup, and stews. I make vegetable stir-frys and dal in my large, straight-sided, lidded sauté pan. To remove greasy or stuck-on bits of food, sprinkle baking soda onto your stainless-steel pots and pans and scrub with a sponge. It works like magic.

Cast iron

This is practically indestructible. If you neglect it, you can pretty easily revive it. It can withstand the flames of a campfire. It will retain the heat of those campfires. And it actually improves with every use.

Before you cook with a cast-iron pan for the first time, you must season it. Until you have added a good seasoning to it, you can't cook acidic foods in it, such as tomato- or wine-based sauces.

To season the pan, wash it with soapy water and dry it, coat it lightly with oil inside and out, wipe the excess oil off with a dedicated cloth, and heat the pan in the oven at 450°F for 30 minutes. Repeat the oiling and heating process a couple of times. The pan will darken and develop a hard layer. By cooking with fat in the pan, you will season it every time you make dinner and render the surface nonstick—without the nonstick chemicals. (If you've bought a pre-seasoned cast-iron pan, you can skip this inaugural seasoning and cook in your pan right away after rinsing it in hot water and drying it.)

I use my skillet to make the usual items you'd find in a frying pan on top of the stove—pancakes, fried eggs, pan-fries and fried potato peels, caramelized onions and shallots—and just about anything you cook in the oven, such as pies, fruit crumbles, sticky buns, galettes, and frittatas. I love to roast vegetables in cast iron; it cleans up so easily. To clean cast iron, wipe it with a sponge, cloth, or brush, or scrub off any sticky bits with a bit of soapy water, if necessary.

I own four cast-iron skillets, ranging from 6 inches to 12 inches in size, and we use at least one or two of these pans every day. I also own two expensive stainless-steel skillets but I prefer my simple—and affordable—cast-iron skillets. To remove any rust that develops, scrub it with a potato and coarse salt, followed by one or two seasonings.

You can sometimes find secondhand cast iron at thrift stores and yard sales. Many people panic when they see a bit of rust on their cast iron and, not knowing how to clean it, ditch their pans. Grab those and nix the nonstick pans. Two of my skillets—one of which is a vintage Griswold!—cost $2 each at an estate sale.

Enameled cast iron

Enameled cast iron features the same beneficial properties as cast iron with the added bonus of a smooth enameled finish inside and out that does not require seasoning and cleans very easily. I use a 6¾-quart Dutch oven to bake sourdough bread and to make soup, stew, chili, baked beans, dal, sauces, and more.

Dutch ovens can go from the stovetop to the oven, they heat evenly, and they retain their heat extremely well. After I make dinner, my pot keeps the food hot on the table while other dishes finish cooking or while everyone dillydallies on the way to the table. With its heat-retaining properties, my small, 2-quart Dutch oven doubles as a yogurt maker, keeping my milk warm as it cultures in a toasty spot in my kitchen or on top of a heating pad set on low. However, sometimes you don't want a pot to retain heat. If you want your food to stop cooking immediately after you remove the heat source, enameled cast-iron pots and pans are not a good choice. They retain heat a little too well.

Enameled cast iron—like all cast iron—is also very heavy. When I describe the dishes I make in my large Dutch oven to my eighty-nine-year-old mother, she always says she would like one. But she would not be able to lift it, empty or full.

To clean enameled cast iron, a soapy sponge will usually do the trick. For baked-on food, let the pot or pan soak or scrub it with baking soda. Do not clean enameled cast iron with steel wool. Speaking of metal, don't use metal utensils in an enameled cast-iron pot or pan, either. They can damage the enamel. Stick with wooden utensils when cooking in enameled cast iron.

Sourdough Tools

Several of the kitchen tools listed here make sourdough bread baking more successful. However, except for the sourdough bread (see page 143) or waffles (see page 150), you'll need only basic kitchen tools to make the other sourdough recipes in this book.

Kitchen scale. Measuring ingredients with a scale will give you accurate readings and more consistent loaves. A thousand grams of flour always weighs a thousand grams—unless we really do move to Mars.

If you measure by volume, a cup of flour will not always be the same amount. Pack the flour down a bit and it might look more like ⅞ cup or even less. Also, you can measure very quickly with a scale—just dump the flour into a bowl on the scale in a few seconds, rather than having to measure it out cup by cup by cup and possibly losing track (was that cup number six or seven?). For this book, I weighed flour on a scale and then used that to measure the volume. I did this several times and on different days. My results by volume varied every time. Get a scale if you will bake sourdough regularly.

Dutch oven. With a Dutch oven, you can replicate the interior of a steam-injecting commercial oven, which creates the sourdough's beautiful, caramelized crust. With its tight-fitting lid, a Dutch oven traps in the moisture released from the dough as it bakes, to create a steamy environment. I have a large 6¾-quart Dutch oven. A 4- or 5-quart pot will suffice. A cast-iron combo cooker also works well.

If you don't have a Dutch oven, bake in loaf pans or on a baking stone or cookie sheet. If desired, place a heatproof dish on the rack beneath the rack the bread bakes on, and fill that dish with water you've boiled. This will create some steam.

Very good oven mitts. You should have these regardless of whether or not you bake sourdough bread. But if you do bake sourdough, you'll handle a pot that has preheated in a 500°F oven.

Dough scraper. Use this to flip your dough around and to clean your work surface. I use my stainless-steel dough scraper every day.

Razor blade or lame. This allows you to score the bread quickly and deeply, releasing it to expand and rise higher in the oven. You can buy these in specialty cooking stores or fashion one *very carefully* out of a razor blade stuck on the end of a wooden stir stick. If you don't have a lame, use a very sharp knife to score your bread.

Banneton baskets. These wicker-like spiral baskets create the ringed pattern on the proofing dough and make it easy to drop that dough into the hot pot. If you don't have these baskets, use a towel-lined bowl sprinkled generously with flour. If you can recruit an extra set of adult hands to carefully hold the towel out of the way when you drop in the dough, do so.

Bread knife. After baking your beautiful rustic loaf of sourdough bread, you don't want to mangle it by slicing into it with your chef's knife.

Grain mill. If you get very serious about baking sourdough bread, consider buying either a small hand-cranked grain mill or an electric grain mill that grinds grains quickly.

Freshly ground winter wheat berries, emmer wheat berries, or rye berries, for example, render absolutely delicious and more nutritious loaves. Many stores that sell bulk food carry these or other varieties of whole grains.

Your freshly ground flour will contain the entire kernel, or seed. Refined flour that you buy at the store has been stripped of the bran and the seed's embryo, or the germ, to render it shelf-stable. These components are rich in protein, vitamins, and minerals. But the germ also contains oils that, once released upon grinding, turn flour rancid quickly, shortening the shelf-life. When you grind flour, try to use it immediately. If things do not go according to plan, store the flour in the refrigerator in a jar and use it as soon as possible.

Fermentation Tools

For all of the fermentation recipes in this book, you will need only basic kitchen equipment, which you most likely already own.

Cutting tools. You need only one good knife to chop vegetables, but you can also use a vegetable grater to shred vegetables or a food processor to speed things up. Just avoid putting onions in a food processor, as the blades render them extremely bitter.

Cutting surface. Personally, I find chopping on a small cutting board frustrating. A good-size cutting board gives you room to work. But if you have only a small cutting board, that will certainly do the job.

Mixing bowls. Plastic and some metal can react with the acids that fermentations produce. Use non-reactive bowls, such as stainless steel, glass, or ceramic. Remember to use a glass bowl for your sourdough starter so you can see the bubbles!

Jars and crocks. I have fermented all sorts of food in simple jars with screw-top lids. However, I really do love bale-top jars with rubber gaskets. They're the Teslas of jars. The tight seal of the rubber gaskets prevents air from entering the jar—and air is what prevents vegetables from fermenting properly. But, truly, just about any jar will do. Because carbon dioxide builds pressure in the jar during active fermentation, avoid explosions by burping—in other words, opening—your jars daily. If you make large vats of sauerkraut, you could treat yourself to a traditional open stoneware crock with weights.

Larger jars that can hold 8 cups or more work well for fermenting beverages, such as the tepache (page 258) and the lemon zesty kombucha (page 255), depending on how much of each drink you'd like to make.

Weights. For vegetables and fruit to ferment properly you must submerge them in liquid. The bacteria that ferment the food are anaerobic and will not reproduce unless you cut off the oxygen (they're kinky little bugs). If you don't submerge your food, it will turn mushy or even moldy on top, which you then scrape off and compost.

Weighting everything down is really the only trick to fermenting food. You can buy special weights for this purpose. I use the jar-within-a-jar method because I have so many free jars and I avoid spending money on single-use gadgets. For sauerkraut, when I pack my jar, I leave a few inches of space at the top. I place a cabbage leaf over that and then place a small, glass, lidless yogurt jar about the height of a large shot glass on top of the cabbage leaf. When I close the jar, the lid shoves down both the little jar and the food, and the liquid rises up to submerge everything perfectly.

Bottles. If you make the kombucha (see page 255) or spicy ginger beer (page 252) in this book, I highly recommend you find some flip-top glass bottles. The tight seal helps build up the carbonation of these drinks. Tepache (page 258) usually has so much carbonation, you won't need a flip-top bottle for it, but you might still want one. If you would prefer a drink with less carbonation, then bottle your drinks in a jar.

When I occasionally brew larger amounts of kombucha in the summer, I will sometimes bottle it in a half-gallon carboy (fancy lingo for "jug"). If you flavor your kombucha with fresh strawberry, which tends to fizz like crazy, even a screw-top bottle should render respectable carbonation.

You can find inexpensive flip-top bottles at beer- and wine-making suppliers. Often beers and sodas packaged in flip-top bottles cost less than empty bottles from a specialty store. Save those, and if your friends buy these drinks, hit them up for their bottles.

- *Bottle accessories.* To fill your bottles, you'll want a funnel. Although you don't want to brew fermented drinks in a metal container, the few milliseconds your drink comes into contact with a metal funnel shouldn't cause any problems. You may also want a bottle brush to clean your bottles.

Optional Tools

- *Tea ball or infuser.* When I brew tea for kombucha, I usually just throw loose-leaf tea in a heat-resistant glass measuring cup and then strain the tea leaves out by pouring the tea through a small sieve. You can also use a tea ball or other infuser. If you have a French press, you can use that to brew tea, the same way you would brew coffee.

- *Wooden pounder.* To make sauerkraut, you need to bruise your vegetables before packing them into jars or leaving them to ferment in an open crock. I simply squeeze the chopped cabbage and whatnot with my hands. For hot peppers, I never do this with bare hands. A wooden pounder is nice to have for this or you can simply weight down the salted hot peppers with something heavy to help bruise them.

Maintain and Repair Your Tools

A zero-waste or low-waste lifestyle can lead to the recovery of several hands-on life skills, such as cooking, gardening, carpentry, DIY, and mending. To make your kitchen tools last, take care of them and repair them when necessary.

Season your cast-iron pans. Don't leave your knives sitting in the bottom of the sink, where they can rust (and cut you). And keep them sharp. Look for a repair shop, a repair cafe, or a handy friend when a small appliance goes on the fritz. Or learn how to repair it yourself. YouTube has a video that shows you how.

Consider secondhand first

We reached peak stuff long ago. When we need something, by choosing secondhand goods over new, we reduce the number of replacement products that a company will manufacture. The secondhand market also stimulates our local economies.

You might be amazed at what you can find at yard sales, thrift shops, and estate sales. Sometimes you may find great stuff just sitting on the curb! Here in the alternate universe of Silicon Valley, where my neighbors kick expensive stuff to the curb constantly, I regularly find treasures by the side of the road. I've scored vintage cast iron, expensive bale-top jars, like-new working small appliances, and solid maple kitchen chairs.

You may find free items in your community through:

• The Buy Nothing Project. Look for a Buy Nothing Facebook group in your city. If your city doesn't have one, consider starting one (buynothingproject.org).

• Craigslist, Nextdoor, Freecycle, Facebook Marketplace, and other community websites (craigslist.org, nextdoor.com, freecycle.org).

• Community swap meets. I have hosted a few of these where I live. At these swaps, not only do we unload still-useful items, we socialize and build community.

If you use an item only occasionally, such as a 15-liter electric coffee urn for your yearly neighborhood block party, you can try renting or borrowing it.

Choose to Reuse:
Cooking Without Disposables

The holy grail of business models is the subscription service. You pay for a service or product month, after month, after month—often even after you no longer want to receive it because you never seem to get around to canceling—until either you or your wallet are completely exhausted, whichever comes first. Subscriptions include your cell phone and internet service, gym memberships, and tangible items like overpackaged delivery boxes for meal kits, Christmas ornament-of-the-month clubs, and throwaway coffee pod-of-the-month clubs.

You may not consider disposable items such as plastic wrap and paper towels as subscriptions, but they essentially are. You buy them, use them, toss them, and then, having grown dependent on them, you must buy more. They may not cost much per package—a couple rolls of paper towels costs only a few dollars—but over time you will spend hundreds of dollars on these, at least. Meanwhile, the alternatives cost very little, if anything.

Alternatives to plastic wrap

Want to cover a bowl of leftovers? Put a plate over it. Need to store half an uneaten melon in the refrigerator? Store it cut side down on a flat plate or pie dish. I store onion halves the same way.

This book includes a recipe for a basic short pastry (page 107) that you can use in several other recipes—a pumpkin pie, a couple of galettes, a pot pie, and the empamosas. In the old days, like most people, I always wrapped the dough tightly in plastic wrap to chill it. Chilling makes rolling out the dough so much easier, but you can chill it without wasting plastic wrap.

Cutting plastic from my life forced me to get creative and develop my revolutionary, pastry-chilling system. Be sure to take notes on this complicated method:

1. Place the pastry on a plate.
2. Cover with a second, inverted plate.

In many cases, a plate as a cover works just as well as plastic wrap, and a turtle really has zero chance of eating your dishes. This trick costs me no extra money and prevents plastic from contaminating my food and contaminating the environment.

Alternatives to plastic baggies

Looking for a way to wrap a sandwich? Try a cloth napkin or use metal sandwich containers or tiffins. The containers cost more upfront, but like other reusable products, they pay for themselves over time because you buy them just once.

In some commercial kitchens, after charring peppers, line cooks then put the steaming hot peppers into a plastic baggie and close it, trapping in the heat and moisture that causes the charred skin to blister. This makes removing the skin with a knife edge very easy. You can skip the baggie and place the hot peppers in a glass, ceramic, metal, cast-iron (i.e., just about anything that isn't plastic) container or a pot with a lid. Or simply put the hot peppers in a bowl and put a plate on top of it.

Yes, washing dishes and containers does consume energy and water. But so do the harvesting, manufacturing, and shipping processes that go into creating each new throwaway product.

Alternatives to parchment paper

You can bring much worse things into your kitchen than parchment paper. I won't judge you if you cling to your parchment paper—or anything else, for that matter. Some companies make unbleached, home-compostable parchment paper. And you can use sheets several times before composting them. But you also have alternatives to expensive parchment paper for cooking pizzas, cakes, cookies, pastries, and more.

For starters, simply grease the baking sheet, cake pan, or baking tin. Yes, you get grease all over you hand. Rub some of that into your skin to help soften your hands. Wipe the rest off with a dish towel rather than a paper towel (that's a bonus example).

Occasionally I dry apple slices in the oven. As they dry out, the apple slices can stick to a cookie sheet without parchment paper. We do own reusable silicone mats, but I really don't like washing these. My solution? I put a cooling rack on my cookie sheet and arrange the apple slices across it. With the warm air of the oven reaching the undersides and tops of the apple slices evenly, they dehydrate quicker than they do if I were to place them directly on the cookie sheet.

If you roast vegetables and want to avoid scrubbing a metal baking sheet or glass dish but also want to avoid using parchment paper, roast your vegetables in cast-iron pans, if you have them since, as I've said, cast iron cleans so easily.

Alternatives to aluminum foil

I love roasted beets and beet pickles. I used to wrap my beets in aluminum foil to roast them in the oven to prevent them from drying out and to keep the roasting dish clean. Occasionally I would save a piece of foil to reuse after unwrapping the beets, but usually I ended up throwing out a bunch of beet juice–covered tinfoil.

Then one day, after I had started to live zero waste, I craved some roasted beets. But how to make them without foil? I wondered if a Dutch oven would work. It did! Had I not imposed the no-foil constraint on myself, I never would have bothered to figure this out. But my beet craving demanded a solution.

Alternatives to coffee pods

No environmentalist worth her package-free salt can write about coffee without the obligatory rant against disposable coffee pods. Not only do they create obscene amounts of waste—Keurig alone sold nearly 10 billion *packs* of pods in 2014—they also represent the Wall·E-fication of our society.

Can we no longer measure out the ground coffee and boil the water? Will we soon need every foodstuff measured and packaged for the specially designed machines that prepare it for us? Personally, I enjoy the ritual of brewing coffee in the morning—or tea. But you can now buy tea pods as well, surely a sign of the endtimes.

Some aluminum coffee pods can be recycled. The problematic combination of plastic and aluminum of many other pods makes them landfill bound. Theoretically, just about everything, with enough effort, energy, and expensive heavy equipment thrown at it, can be recycled. That doesn't mean it will be or should be recycled. And besides, recycling is a last resort. Above all else, refuse trash at its source.

For a no-waste method of brewing coffee, which takes all of 5 minutes to prepare a couple of cups, brew in a French press. If you worry you will never recover those 5 minutes of your life, do something productive while you wait for your caffeine hit—put some dishes away, feed the cat, talk to your partner. Toss the spent coffee grounds directly on the soil around your plants outside. My roses especially love the acidic grounds.

Alternatives to tea bags

Fabric and mesh tea bags are often made of synthetic material—in other words, plastic. Landfill concerns aside, you don't want to eat or drink something after it has been heated in plastic. When you heat food—or tea leaves—in plastic, nasty chemicals can leach into what you're about to consume. Even paper tea bags may contain small amounts of plastic in the sealant. And most tea bags—synthetic or paper—are individually wrapped, then stuffed into a box that is often wrapped in yet more plastic.

Loose-leaf tea generally costs less than tea bags and tastes better. Fill a tea ball for an individual cup or brew it in a teapot for a crowd. You can also use a French press. Like coffee grounds, the spent tea leaves can go directly onto the soil around your plants. You can, of course, compost these, as well as coffee grounds.

Alternatives to paper towels

My mother—who grew up without paper towels—wonders how I live without them.

But we have many alternatives to single-use paper towels. I have a lifetime supply of cotton rags I cut from my kids' old tee-shirts. I keep them in a jar for cleaning up. I also sewed a dozen "unpaper towels" from a worn-out flannel sheet; that is, I cut out flannel rectangles the size of standard paper towels and finished the edges. When these get dirty, I wash them. For bigger spills, which don't happen that often, I clean up with a dish towel or flour-sack towel; hang that up somewhere to dry, such as outside over a metal chair; and wash it later with the other towels.

When people hear that I don't buy paper towels, one of their first questions is "But how do you drain fried food?!" To drain fried food, you can keep one towel dedicated for that task. When you're done, quickly wash it by hand to spare your laundry the extra grease. You can also drain the fried food by placing it on a cooling rack set on a cookie sheet. When the fat has hardened and cooled, remove it and set it aside. Season cast-iron pans with that fat or, if your city collects food waste, place the fat in the proper collection receptacle.

The benefit of always having to do all the shopping yourself, because no one else wants to do it, which can greatly annoy you, is that you control what comes into your home. Chances are, others can not be bothered going to the store to buy these disposable products, and they will make do with what they find in the kitchen. Sometimes procrastination and apathy work to your advantage.

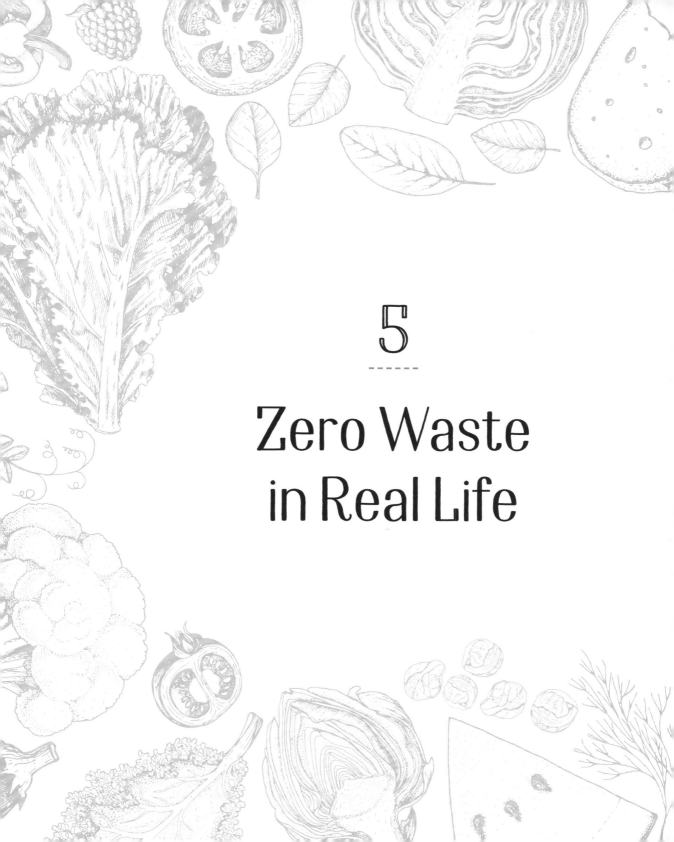

5

- - - - - -

Zero Waste
in Real Life

"Zero-waste living costs too much."

"I can't afford the gear I need to live zero waste."

"I'll reduce my waste once I've saved up enough money to buy all the zero-waste stuff I need to replace all my existing stuff that I'll then throw out."

One of the misgivings I hear about living zero waste is that it costs too much money. But trust me when I say this lifestyle should save you money, not bankrupt you. You don't need to buy all kinds of fancy gear—new matching jars for your pantry, new matching wooden crates to house the new matching jars, special utensils designed specifically for eating out (food is food), and so on. To buy more stuff defeats the purpose. Zero waste is not a consumer lifestyle. It's a conserver lifestyle.

Yes, some lower-waste options cost more, such as milk sold in refillable glass bottles versus milk sold in plastic jugs, or local produce from the farmers' market versus produce from a discount grocery store. But other aspects of this lifestyle will save you money: buying in bulk (for many items, not all), eating every morsel of the food you buy, eating lower on the food chain, and eating more home-cooked meals.

And some necessities that make low-waste living possible need not cost much, if anything at all, such as your zero-waste kit: the "equipment" you'll use when buying groceries, packing lunches, or eating out.

The chic, minimalist, zero-waste gear looks tempting, and you may want to buy some of it, but you don't need to buy all of it. We can't shop our way out of the climate crisis.

Your Zero-Waste Kit Works Like a Shield to Deflect Unwanted Single-Use Trash

Insulated at home, I easily feed myself and my family without generating waste. All I need to cook dal, for example, are onions, garlic, lentils, tomatoes, and spices—ingredients that one of us brought home without packaging—and voilà: a tasty, satisfying, and inexpensive dinner.

After we eat our comfort food, nothing makes its way into the trash because we eat our leftovers and, of course, we don't set the table with throwaway Styrofoam plates, plastic cutlery, and takeaway coffee cups. But when I venture forth into the "real world," which is filled with Styrofoam and plastic, I need to be prepared. I arm myself with both a zero-waste kit and a ready response for well-intended servers, store clerks, and anyone else who tries to hand me stuff I don't want. I'll repeat one word, often: "no." Actually, I'll repeat: "no, thank you," because I may as well be polite.

When you reduce your waste, you learn to say "no" often, a useful life skill in and of itself, but that's a topic for another book. Many women—the majority of my readers—find saying "no" difficult. As you continue on your low-waste journey, this step will become easier, especially if you equip yourself with the basic gear.

If you've never ordered food in your own container and you want to try it but feel self-conscious or embarrassed about making such an overtly subversive request— "Please put my food here"—call in reinforcements by way of a hungry, container-wielding friend who also wants a sandwich.

On-the-Go Essentials

You may want a couple of kits—one for shopping and one for taking on the go. If you have bundled a long shopping trip with several errands, bring both kits. When you get hungry, you can treat yourself to a cup of tea or a snack, and enjoy them waste-free.

Look around your home for the following items. You probably already own many of them. Once you have gathered your equipment, packing your kits takes all of 5 minutes. If you walk or ride your bike everywhere, keep your kits packed and ready to go near your front door or in a front hall closet. If you drive, keep your gear in your car.

Grocery shopping kit

• Shopping bags   • Produce bags   • Jars or containers

Out-and-about kit

• One bag to hold everything   • Water bottle   • Cloth napkin   • Produce bag
   • Utensils   • Jar or metal container

When you return home, clean any dirty items in your kit, repack the items, and have them ready to go for your next sortie.

Cloth Shopping Bags

Americans consume 100 billion single-use plastic shopping bags every year. On the bright side, the 400-plus recent laws either banning or taxing plastic bags in cities and states throughout the country have motivated many customers to dutifully carry their reusable shopping bags with them everywhere or to question if they need a bag at all. (If you grab just one thing at the store, do you really need a bag for it?) Near me in San Jose, for example, shortly after the city imposed its Bring Your Own Bag Ordinance in 2012, single-use plastic bag debris decreased by 89 percent in storm drains and 60 percent in creeks and rivers.

Bag bans work.

However, not all reusable shopping bags are equal. Many of the reusable shopping bags on the market are made of synthetic materials, such as polyester, nylon, and rayon—in other words, plastic. When these synthetic bags go through the washing machine, they release plastic microfibers. At 5mm long or less and with a diameter measured in micrometers (1/1000th of a millimeter), these tiny plastic microfibers easily pass through the filters of washing machines, subsequently polluting our rivers, lakes, and oceans—and our food chain. One study estimates that 1.4 million trillion microfibers pollute the seafloor.

When choosing shopping bags, look for those made with natural fibers. Canvas or heavy-duty cotton work well and will last for years.

Cloth Produce and Bulk Bin Bags

Although bans and taxes on plastic shopping bags help reduce the amount of single-use plastic entering the environment, they do not address the massive amounts of single-use plastic we put into the bags in the form of produce bags. Some stores and farmers' markets now offer compostable produce bags, often with the caveat "compostable where facilities exist." In many places, these facilities do not exist. Calling these types of bags compostable is like calling all lottery tickets "winnable where crystal balls exist."

Other compostable bags *do* completely disintegrate in a backyard composter, leaving behind only carbon dioxide and biomass, with the help of microorganisms present in the soil. Greenwashing can make distinguishing among the different types of bags difficult, and terms like *biodegradable* further add to the confusion. Biodegradable plastic bags break down into smaller pieces of plastic that do not completely disappear.

But even if you manage to decipher the claims on bags and choose compostable ones that decompose completely and quickly in a home compost pile, such single-use bags still waste resources. The raw materials that go into the bags must be grown, often from corn or other crops that could feed people and that require land, water, and chemical inputs. This raw material then must be harvested, shipped to a manufacturing plant via trucks or rail or ship, manufactured into bags, packaged, distributed to wholesalers and stores, used by the consumer once, and, finally, composted.

"Compostable where facilities exist" perpetuates a linear, unsustainable system of consumption—a straight line that begins at a farm and ends at a commercial composting facility, a landfill, incinerator, or the ocean.

Reusable cloth produce bags, on the other hand, while undergoing similar steps to manufacture as compostable-where-facilities-exist bags, once created, can then be used hundreds or even thousands of times.

Back in 2011, my daughter MK and I sewed very simple cloth produce bags in the same size and shape as the plastic ones available in the produce aisles of stores. I still use these today. I stash them in my cloth shopping bags so I always have them on hand.

I use these bags for buying fruit and vegetables at the farmers' market and for filling up on certain bulkier items at the bulk bins, such as beans, rice, grains, pasta, oats, dried fruit, nuts, and, occasionally, chocolate. When my bags get dirty, I toss them in the washing machine, where they take up very little space. I use about eight bags a week, which replace 416 plastic bags every year. Now a decade later, that number has added up to 4,160 bags for one family.

Most of us adjusted quickly to carrying reusable shopping bags with us. Some of us switched out of a desire to be more environmentally conscious, and some of us switched out of necessity when our cities banned plastic shopping bags or taxed them. We can also quickly adjust to shopping with reusable produce bags. The plastic produce bag bans will come and, in fact, they have already started where I live in Northern California. We can be cutting-edge and voluntarily make the switch now.

Beyond fruit, vegetables, and bulk: Uses for cloth produce bags

• **Buy loose bread.** Some grocery stores and bakeries stock their loaves, rolls, bagels, pastries, and so on loose in a bin or display case. Put your selection in a cloth produce bag. If a clerk waits on you behind a counter, hand over the clean cloth bag when placing your order and explain that you'd like the food directly in the bag.

- **Store bread.** I freeze whole loaves of sourdough bread in cloth produce bags for about two weeks at the most. I never slice them first as they can become dried out and freezer burned. I store bread on the counter in these bags also.

- **Pack a sandwich.** You won't want to pack a very juicy sandwich with lots of mayonnaise and juicy pickles but, rather, sandwiches like peanut butter and jam or hummus and cheese.

- **Pack a doggy bag.** Restaurants often bring more bread to the table than diners can eat. Ditto with the tortilla chips at Mexican restaurants. These are very difficult to find in bulk. Grab them while you can!

- **Spin-dry fresh greens.** Wash greens, place them in a clean bag, take the bag outside, and twirl it around a bunch of times to dry the greens off. Store the damp bag in the crisper. Unlike a salad spinner, a produce bag will take up no space in your kitchen.

PRODUCE-BAG SEWING BEES

In 2018, I started organizing produce-bag sewing bees with a handful of amazing volunteers where I live. We sew bags out of donated, unwanted fabric that may otherwise go to a landfill, and we give these bags away. Since we began, we have handed out thousands of these cloth produce bags at one of our local farmers' markets.

But we don't just give people an alternative to plastic. These cloth produce bags start conversations about plastic pollution. They're like a gateway reusable item, and shoppers we speak with start thinking about other plastic they can eliminate from their lives. They may also start to complain to businesses about their excessive packaging, or sign petitions, or contact their elected representatives to demand support for bans on single-use plastic. All of that from a bit of cloth!

To look for a produce-bag sewing group or to add your group to a map I maintain of groups around the world, go to zerowastechef.com/reusa-bags.

Make it: Homemade cloth produce and bulk bags

You can buy cloth produce bags from some grocery stores and health food co-ops, or online from Life Without Plastic (lifewithoutplastic.com) or Package Free (package-freeshop.com). But if you have a bit of fabric, a sewing machine, and a few minutes, you can also make some.

Cut out some rectangles about 23 inches by 18 inches. Fold each rectangle in half like a book. Sew the bottom and side. Finish the top with a hem or overlock stitch.

If you have a scale, you can weigh your bags and mark the weights on them (i.e., the "tares"). If you choose somewhat heavy fabric or cut down pillow cases that have a thick, heavy finished border and piping, you'll want to mark the tare somehow.

To weigh your bag, put it on a digital scale. If you've set the scale to measure in ounces, divide the weight by 16 (the number of ounces in a pound). That's your tare. If you've chosen grams, divide the number on your scale by 454. My cloth bags typically weigh around 1.12 ounces. The tare is 1.12/16 = 0.07.

You can write the tare on the fabric with a permanent marker or embroider it on if your sewing machine has that feature.

If you want to be able to close your bags, add a casing in the top of your bag for a drawstring. Or pin two equal lengths of lightweight ribbon to one side of the bag and sew them into the side seam. Use these to tie the bag shut. And if all else fails, just tie off the top of your bags with an elastic hairband or a rubber band. Or just buy the damn bags. You don't have to do everything on your own.

Glass Jars

The humble glass jar symbolizes zero-waste living for good reason. You'll use glass jars constantly for many tasks.

Shopping at bulk bins

Get the weight marked on your jars before you fill them up. You want to pay for the weight of the food in the jar only, not the weight of the food in the jar plus the weight of the jar, because when you buy tea at $48 per pound, you really don't want the jar's extra ounces tallied in the total weight.

At some stores, customer service associates will weigh jars for you and mark the tare on them. You can use a china marker to directly mark the jar and not waste any stickers or tape. Look for these in art supply stores. Other stores set out scales, and you weigh the jars yourself. At yet other stores, the staff may appear completely bewildered when you bring in your jars. Be patient! The employees are still getting used to customers shopping this way.

After you fill up your jars with bulk foods, the cashier will deduct the weight of the jar from the total weight of the filled jar so you pay for the weight of the food only.

Shopping for delicate berries

In the summer, I also take a few jars to the farmers' market for filling with berries. This way I bring home whole fruit rather than jam.

Food laws vary, but here in Northern California, after I (gently) dump berries into a jar and return the baskets to the vendor while I'm at the booth, the vendor can reuse the baskets. If I take them home and return them later, the vendor cannot reuse them until after steaming them with a very expensive piece of equipment that no one owns. The thinking behind this law is that the baskets become contaminated in our homes.

I may look like a bit of a weirdo carefully transferring berries to my jars at the farmers' market, but I'm pretty okay with that.

When I get back home, I freeze some of my berries. I pour water into one or two of the jars, swish around the berries to clean them, cut them in half, spread them on a cookie sheet, freeze them, then transfer them back to that jar I brought them home in and put that in the freezer. This reduces the number of dishes I have to wash.

Packing leftovers and lunches

When you eat out, fill a jar in your out-and-about kit with leftovers that you can take to work the next day for lunch. After you eat your leftovers, bring home any compost in the emptied jar. It's the circle of food! Although glass jars work well for the grownups' lunches, opt for metal containers for kids.

Water Bottle

If you don't have a metal water bottle for hydrating on the go, use a mason jar with a tight-fitting lid that doesn't leak. Fill it with water or order your coffee or tea to go in your jar. Wrap several rubber bands around the outside of the hot jar or slip the jar into a small sock so you don't burn your hand.

Utensils

Again, save money and conserve resources by using what you already have rather than buying special utensils. Nothing matches? Great! You have an eclectic set of utensils. Everyone has metal utensils at home. If you keep a fork, spoon, and knife packed in your out-and-about kit, you'll never have to use disposable plastic cutlery again. Tuck a pair of chopsticks in there, too.

Cloth Napkins

Wrap a sandwich up furoshiki style and have your wrapping and napkin all in one. Lay your sandwich in the center of a large napkin. Bring two opposite corners together and tie them over the sandwich. Tie the remaining two corners the same way. Your sandwich is packed and ready to travel.

Metal Tiffins and Lunch Containers

These cost more upfront than single-use plastic sandwich bags, but they pay for themselves and kids won't break them at school.

Perfect Is Not an Option

Occasionally, you may bring home contraband. Plastic happens. A well-meaning store clerk may wrap your containers in plastic. Another clerk may refuse to fill your containers—when just last week a different clerk at the same store not only did so but also thanked you for your efforts! The cheese you used to buy at the deli in your own container is now only available in vacuum-packed plastic pouches and your three-year-old really wants his favorite cheese *right now*!

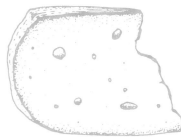

These dilemmas can send a zero waster over the edge. Don't beat yourself up over mishaps. The majority of our stores and our food system are not yet designed for this type of conscious shopping, which used to be the norm. However, with a little planning, anyone can reduce the waste he or she brings home.

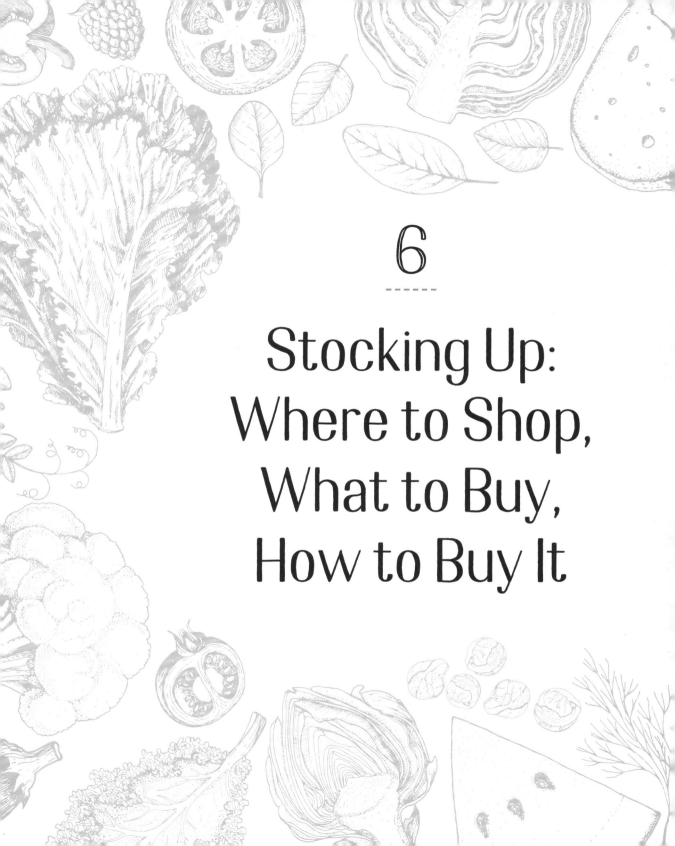

6

Stocking Up: Where to Shop, What to Buy, How to Buy It

Before I broke up with plastic, if I craved a snack I'd grab a handful (or two or three) of crackers from a plastic-lined box or I might grab a biscotti from a plastic tray housed inside a plastic bag. Today, if I want to eat a little something I'll choose a piece of fruit or, if I've baked any, some sourdough graham crackers (see page 244). Although baking these crackers doesn't require that much effort, opening a box requires none. As a result, I eat fewer crackers and appreciate them more. This is not deprivation. This is treating my body well. And the crackers taste much better.

When you stop buying the shiny packages of highly processed food, you have no other choice but to eat more whole foods—fruit and vegetables, legumes, nuts and seeds, and whole grains. These foods also happen to fall lower on the food chain and result in fewer emissions than foods that are higher up there, such as beef and dairy.

Moving up the food chain, if you drink milk, look for it in returnable, refillable glass bottles. I can choose milk and even raw milk from among several dairies that sell their milk this way. More and more dairies package their milk in glass, but availability varies. Depending on where you live, a local dairy may even deliver milk in glass bottles that it later picks up, just like in the old days. As for cheese, some cheese or deli counters will fill your clean container with it.

Our dairy and our eggs come from pasture-raised, rotationally grazed animals that roam around outside and do what animals were meant to do—graze the land, eat the diet nature intended, and nourish the soil with their manure. I pay much more for this food because raising animals humanely while stewarding the land requires more labor and more space than a concentrated animal feeding operation (CAFO) does. In a CAFO, thousands of animals are brutally crammed together as they stand in their filth that automated equipment eventually drains and pipes out into nearby cesspools that foul the land, water, and air. I'll pay extra, thanks. And the money my zero-waste lifestyle saves me more than covers the price of my pastured eggs.

What to Buy

Key ingredients for a zero-waste kitchen

Between the farmers' market and bulk stores, I can buy everything I need package-free. Although my fresh produce varies by season, I stock the same key groups year-round.

To simplify my life, I try to stock ingredients that can become other ingredients. Cream of tartar combined with baking soda makes baking powder. Cane sugar combined with molasses makes brown sugar. Of course, don't feel obligated to make your own baking powder and brown sugar. But if you need some in a pinch and have the other basic building blocks, you can easily prep some.

I stock my kitchen with food from the following main categories:

- Fresh vegetables
- Fresh fruit
- Fresh herbs
- Legumes
- Nuts and seeds
- Grains
- Rice
- Pasta
- Pastured dairy and eggs
- Dry herbs and spices
- Pantry staples
- Dried fruit
- Baking supplies
- Coffee and tea

Where to Shop

You've assembled your zero-waste shopping kit, you've decided what to cook based on the food you have on hand, and you've compiled a shopping list of missing ingredients. You'll now attempt your first low-waste shopping trip.

With a shopping list in hand, you will not only avoid all those plastic-wrapped impulse buys at the front of the checkout, but you'll also know just how many reusable bags, jars, and containers you'll need to take with you shopping. A little bit of planning will help you eliminate a great deal of waste.

On this inaugural trip, you'll probably notice plastic everywhere *because plastic is everywhere.* The center aisles especially of the grocery store are a plastic minefield.

You may wonder, as I did starting out on my low-waste quest, how you'll ever avoid the plastic packages. Take heart! We did not adjust to a new shopping routine overnight. We had to figure out which stores had the best bulk options—and which would allow us to fill up using our own containers. We had to plan ahead more. And with our closest farmers' market running only on Sundays, we had to get more organized.

Local, seasonal, organic, and other modifiers

Several generations ago, food didn't suffer from adjectivitis. We simply called food *food.* Today, plastic not only provides packaging for shelf-stable food, but it also provides real estate for marketing lingo such as "gluten-free" on foods that obviously have never contained gluten; "natural," which could mean just about anything; and supposed improvements such as "Now with real juice!"

Other adjectives have more meaning. Buying seasonally grown food from local, independent farmers and family grocers benefits your community. According to Indie-Bound, an association of independent local bookstores, when you shop at a small, local business, for every $100 you spend, $52 stays in the community. Spend $100 with the big guys, and a paltry $13 remains in your community. Spend that $100 online remotely, and no money stays in your community. No sales taxes are collected to pay for funding schools and keeping hospitals open and paying firefighters. Local businesses also create local jobs. Those employees go on to spend their paychecks in the community.

Local food travels fewer miles to get to you, resulting in higher nutrition and lower transport emissions. It requires less packaging. It tastes better. Unless we want to buy every morsel of food from giant corporate supermarkets, we'd better support the small guys so they stay in business.

Organic often costs more. Even if you don't believe it benefits you, it does benefit the farmers who grow it by reducing their exposure to pesticides. It also benefits the soil they grow it in. If you don't usually buy organic produce, you may want to splurge on it for ingredients in any of the many recipes in this book that call for peels or citrus zest, such as the Save-Scraps-Save-Cash Vegetable Broth (page 135), Apple Scrap Vinegar (page 101), and Preserved Lemons (page 95), as peels and skins often harbor the most pesticide residues. Some citrus also has a shiny wax food-grade coating. Ask your grocer if the citrus has been treated with this if you'd rather avoid it. None of the farmers at my farmers' market apply this wax to the organic citrus they grow and sell.

Good, Better, Best Zero-Waste Shopping

I regularly hear from people here in the United States and around the world who have no access to either farmers' markets or bulk bins, and they feel terribly guilty for buying food in plastic packages. Do not feel guilty for a supply chain that you did not create. You must eat. Just do your best.

Here in temperate Northern California, we can buy unpackaged local fruit and vegetables year-round at our outdoor farmers' markets; some of our bulk stores actually encourage shoppers to bring their own reusable bags and containers to fill up; and the majority of grocery stores stock milk and cream in returnable, refillable glass bottles. Today—now that I have the routine down—I don't find living zero-waste here all that difficult. (Also, I can wear Birkenstocks almost every day of the year, and yes, I wear Birkenstocks.)

If you don't have access to similar shopping options, you can reduce your waste in other ways.

GOOD

Produce

With no access to farmers' markets, try these strategies:

- **Shop with reusable produce bags.** Take reusable cloth produce bags to the grocery store for buying produce. Fill your bags with loose apples, carrots, potatoes, and so on. Buy greens such as bunches of spinach and romaine lettuce rather than those prepped in plastic bags. Save all the stems for vegetable broth.

- **Remember that some items don't need a produce bag.** A bunch of bananas, a couple of onions, or a squash can go directly into your shopping cart and then into your shopping bag.

- **Join a CSA (community supported agriculture) and request no plastic.** Some CSAs use less packaging than others. Ask around. If your CSA wraps its food with lots of plastic packaging, when you return your box, return the packaging along with it and include a note explaining why. In the United States, you can find a CSA near you through Local Harvest (localharvest.org).

Pantry staples

If you don't have a good bulk store near you, here's what you can do to reduce your product-to-packaging ratio:

- **Buy giant packages of food.** If you and your family will eat 25 pounds of rice, then buy the 25-pound bag of rice. Yes, you'll have a large package to dispose of. But keep in mind that the foods in the bulk bins also arrived at the store in giant packages. The staff doesn't grow the rice out in the parking lot.

- **Split giant packages of food with friends and neighbors.** When you pitch this idea to your friends and neighbors, explain that they will save not only money but also time, as only one person will have to do the actual shopping and schlepping. Plus, when you all get together to split the goods, you can make a party of it (woo-hoo!). You may even start your own buying club and purchase large packages of food from a wholesaler.

BETTER

Produce

If your city has one: Shop at the farmers' market. I go to the farmers' market almost every weekend. I find it outrageous that in Northern California—where farms abound—I cannot find a local apple at most of our grocery stores. The apples in those stores travel from Washington State or Canada. Plus, they have those annoying produce stickers stuck to them. Produce at my farmers' market has very little packaging to speak of, it tastes better than anything I can buy in a store, and I enjoy varieties of fruit and vegetables I won't find in a grocery store. I can also buy "ugly" fruits and vegetables that most supermarkets refuse to carry, which helps reduce food waste. More of my money goes directly to the farmers, which helps them stay in business. Remember to bring your zero-waste shopping kit.

- -

NO COUPONS AT THE FARMERS' MARKET

How often do you see a coupon for a carrot, cabbage, or cauliflower? Most coupons at the grocery store offer discounts for highly processed food. When you buy real food like fresh produce, you don't have to worry as much about overpaying. A store—even an upscale market—really can charge only so much for an apple. Once a food manufacturer has processed that apple into, say, applesauce or fruit snacks, the price skyrockets no matter where you buy it. Stick to the whole apple, save money.

- -

Pantry staples

If you do have access to bulk bins, but the store won't allow you to use your own containers and produce bags:

- **Reuse the store's plastic bags.** If the store insists you must use its plastic bags for bulk shopping, and you reuse those bags over and over, how will anyone ever know if you don't use a new bag every time? I'm just asking.

- **Complain.** It amazes me that some shops just flat-out refuse to allow customers to bring their own bags and containers. Don't they want our money? Is business so good that they can afford to turn it away? If you speak with store management, explain to them that they will buy fewer plastic bags and save money if they allow people to bring their own bags.

BEST

Produce

Whether you live in a cold or warm climate:

- **Extend the season.** For example, near the end of summer, when you can buy piles of tomatoes cheaply, you can preserve them in a number of ways.

  - *Roast and freeze tomatoes.* Every summer, I buy two or three or four 20-pound cases of tomatoes. I roast the tomatoes and freeze them to cook with throughout the winter (see page 121).

  - *Make and freeze tomato paste or pizza sauce.* You'll be so happy come January to find your sauce in the back of the freezer (see pages 122 and 227).

  - *Ferment tomatoes.* Follow the same method as for the tomato salsa, but prep only tomatoes and omit the other vegetables. Store these in the refrigerator or, if you have one, a cold cellar.

  - *Dehydrate tomatoes.* I've dehydrated tomatoes in a solar food dryer and they taste like candy. They actually are candy. I would keep them through the winter, but we eat them all because they taste so good. You can dehydrate these in the oven on a very low temperature.

  - *Can tomatoes.* Put up a several mason jars' worth and enjoy tomatoes all winter long.

- **Grow some food.** Grow it at home or grow it together with friends and neighbors in small community gardens and orchards. Not everyone can do this (or wants to), but when you grow your own, you become more self-reliant, you save money, your food tastes delicious, you teach your children valuable life-long skills, you reduce your waste, and your food travels feet, rather than miles, to reach your table. Gardening also provides cheap therapy. If you can also keep chickens, you'll never buy eggs again.

Pantry staples

If you have access to bulk bins in a store that allows you to bring your own reusable containers and bags, then you can:

- **Fill your jars with zero-waste abandon.** It's worth repeating: Be sure to have your jars or other containers tared—in other words, weighed—before you fill them with food.

  - I'm lucky enough to live close to bulk stores with very good selections. I can buy hard-to-find items such as: baker's yeast, miso paste in a dozen flavors, handmade tofu, maple syrup, bee pollen, gochugaru (for kimchi), nigari powder (for making tofu), pasta, molasses, honey, cooking oils of all kinds, chocolate chips, dried mushrooms, tea and dried herbs and spices of all kinds, fermented pickles and kimchi and sauerkraut, dried seaweed, and personal-care products like shampoo and conditioner and henna.

  - Every few months, I buy a large haul. I'll take a total of twenty to twenty-five reusables to fill up, both jars and my produce-cum-bulk-bin bags. Some stores will deduct 5 cents off my bill for each reusable, plus my shopping bags (I'll use four). So for a typical haul, I'll save between $1.00 and $1.25.

  - If that minimal amount of money doesn't persuade you to try bulk shopping, then think of all the trash you'll divert from a landfill. If I buy even twenty items in packaging as I had done before my awakening, I would have eventually thrown away at least twenty pieces of trash but probably more, as I buy large amounts of some items that would require at least a couple of bags or boxes. And most of that packaging would have consisted of plastic, which never breaks down.

- -

FIND A BULK STORE NEAR YOU

Search for bulk stores worldwide at zerowastehome.com/app.
Users can also submit stores not yet listed on this web-based app.

- -

7

You Can Make That? Staples and Scraps

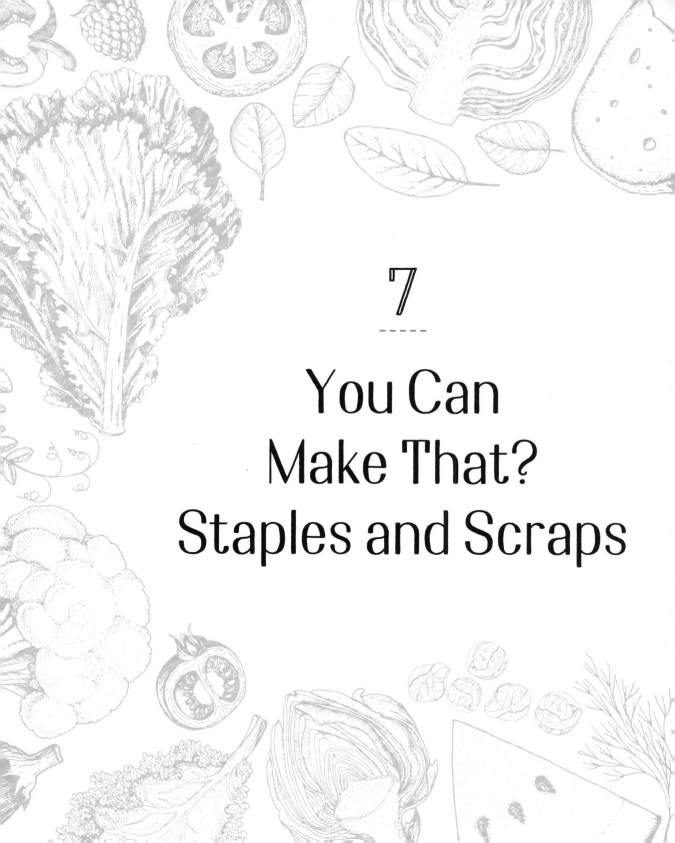

Pick-Your-Peppers Hot Sauce

Like most fermented foods, this hot pepper sauce requires little hands-on prep. Essentially, you chop and salt the peppers, weight them down for an hour or so to draw out their juices, and then pack them into clean jars. Wait a month or so, whirl them in a blender with some vinegar (see page 101), and voilà! Delicious hot sauce filled with beneficial living cultures.

The types of peppers you choose for your sauce depend on availability and your heat tolerance. I can easily find jalapeños and serranos at my farmers' market. If you feel more adventurous, add some habaneros or—if you dare—Scotch bonnets. Other hot choices include the cayenne pepper and chile de árbol varieties. Fresno peppers offer heat similar to jalapeños. Poblanos add only a mild kick.

Taste the prepped peppers before packing them into your jar. If you went a little overboard with the spice, mix in some chopped bell peppers to temper the heat. There is no shame in admitting that you can't handle Scotch bonnets.

Makes about 1½ cups

1 bell pepper, plus more as needed

1 pound hot peppers, such as Fresno, habanero, jalapeño, or serrano, tops removed

2 teaspoons salt

6 garlic cloves, minced

¼ cup apple cider vinegar, strong Apple Scrap Vinegar (page 101), or kombucha vinegar (see page 255), plus more to taste

Remove the top and seeds from the bell pepper. Reserve the top and set aside.

Chop the hot peppers and bell pepper roughly into ½-inch pieces or run them through a food processor. Do not remove the seeds.

In a bowl, mix the chopped peppers, the salt, and garlic. Taste. If the mixture is too hot, add more chopped bell peppers.

Place a small plate inside the bowl, directly on top of the pepper mixture. Place a weight on the plate (a jug of water will do). Cover the weight and bowl completely with a towel. This weight will help draw juices out of the peppers. Set aside for an hour or two, until you see that a large pool of liquid has formed in the bottom of the bowl.

recipe continues ⤞

←« recipe continued from previous page

With a wooden spoon or pounder—never use your hand when packing peppers!—pack the peppers into a jar large enough to leave 3 or 4 inches of headspace at the top. Pour any liquid from the bowl into the jar.

Place the reserved top of the bell pepper over the peppers in the jar. If you have one, place a small jar or other weight on the bell pepper top. When you close the lid of the large jar, the small jar will push down the bell pepper top and all the vegetables, submerging them in liquid. If necessary, add a small amount of water to submerge the peppers. Place the jar on a plate to catch any liquid that bubbles out during active fermentation, which usually begins around day 2 or 3. Open the jar daily during this active period to release the carbon dioxide building up in the jar.

Set the jar aside at room temperature. After about 4 weeks, smell and taste a small piece of a pepper. It should smell and taste sour. I like to use these fermented peppers to garnish cauliflower and potato dal (page 217), chana masala (page 197), and more. You may want to squirrel some away in the refrigerator in a small jar with a bit of the liquid.

Place the contents of the jar in a food processor or high-speed blender. Add the vinegar and process until smooth. If desired, add more vinegar for a thinner sauce.

Pour the sauce into a clean bottle and store it in the refrigerator, where it will keep for over 1 year.

Note

Be careful when preparing hot peppers! Before chopping them, I rub oil onto my hands to create a barrier that helps prevent the capsaicin—the oil in hot peppers that gives them their kick—from burning my skin. But don't rub on so much oil that you can no longer handle a knife safely. And learn from my mistake: Never rub your eyes or nose after prepping hot peppers! If you do, soak a cloth in milk and apply the cloth to your eye.

And now for your next recipe . . .

When you have just a bit of hot pepper sauce remaining in the jar, pour in some olive oil, close the lid tightly and shake the jar to combine. Use your hot and spicy oil for sautéing anything you'd like to add some heat to, such as the onions for a savory dish, stir fry vegetables, or scrambled eggs.

Preserved Lemons

The process of fermentation renders intense flavors. It puts the sour in sweet-and-sour kombucha, the tang in tomato salsa, and the pickle in "pickled" peppers. But of all the fermented recipes in this book, preserved lemons pack the most piquancy per morsel (PPM).

If you have a jar, some salt, access to a lemon tree, and a propensity toward neglect—these sit for a month or longer—you can make this premium kitchen staple yourself for free. If you buy lemons, you'll want to avoid pesticides and waxes, since you make these for the prized rinds (but can eat the pulp also).

Scrub the lemons well. Cut 6 of the lemons into quarters, leaving about ½ inch intact at the bottom to keep the quarters attached to each other. Stuff 1 tablespoon salt into a cut lemon and stuff the lemon into a clean 1-quart jar. Repeat with the remaining 5 split lemons. Leave about 3 inches of space at the top of the jar.

Juice the remaining 4 lemons and pour the juice into the jar until you have completely covered the lemons. Packed tightly into the jar, the lemons should not float to the top, but if you have a weight or a small glass bowl, place that on top to submerge the lemons in the juice. Close the jar and set it on a plate to catch any lemon juice that may gurgle out of the jar during fermentation. Burp the jar (i.e., open it) every day for the first several days to release developing gases. Set the jar aside at room temperature for 1 month.

The lemons are ready when the skins have softened. They will keep for at least 1 year in the refrigerator.

Makes 6 preserved lemons

10 lemons

6 tablespoons sea salt

Spices of choice, if desired, such as 1 bay leaf, 3 or 4 whole cloves, 5 or 6 coriander seeds, 5 or 6 black peppercorns, 1 cinnamon stick

And now for your next recipe . . .

When your preserved lemons have softened, make hummus (page 248) and the farro and kale salad (page 204). Chopped up, the lemons make a potent garnish for the cauliflower and potato dal (page 217) and the chana masala (page 197). When you run out of the lemons themselves, hold on to the juice in the bottom of the jar and use it to flavor dishes and to make dressings.

Soft Burger Buns

Unlike the other bread recipes in this book, these soft burger buns call for commercial baker's yeast rather than sourdough starter. Commercial yeast produces consistent loaves without the need for a sourdough starter to take care of. This dependability led to commercial yeast—not long after scientists developed it in the late 1800s—usurping wild yeast's millennia-long dominance as *the* leavening agent for bread. And while I'll never denigrate the wild yeast of sourdough, I will admit that you won't need to take notes when learning to bake with this simpler yeast, except for perhaps a note to double the recipe because these soft buns taste amazing.

Combine the milk, water, and butter in a small saucepan. Heat until the butter just melts. Cool to 105°F to 110°F. At this temperature, the mixture will be warm—but not hot—to the touch.

While the mixture cools, whisk together the yeast, salt, sugar, and 2¼ cups of the flour in a large bowl.

Stir the milk mixture into the dry ingredients. Add the egg. Mix everything well until combined.

Add the remaining 2 cups flour, ½ cup at a time, mixing well after each addition.

Form the dough into a ball and turn out onto a floured surface. Knead for about 7 minutes, until smooth and elastic. Place in a greased bowl, turn the dough over to lightly grease all sides, and cover with a dish towel. Let rest for 1 hour in a warm spot, until doubled in size.

Punch down the dough, place on a floured work surface, and with a sharp knife or dough scraper, divide into 12 pieces. Roll each piece into a ball. With your thumbs, pull the sides down toward the bottom of the ball, pinching the bottom. Rotate and continue to pull and pinch the dough until you have formed a smooth ball. Flatten the ball slightly.

Makes 12 buns

¾ cup (175 ml) whole or 2% milk

¾ cup (175 ml) water or whey leftover from making ricotta (see page 117)

¼ cup (½ stick; 57 g) unsalted butter, plus more for greasing the cookie sheets

2¼ teaspoons (7 g) active dry yeast

1½ teaspoons (8 g) salt

2 tablespoons (25 g) sugar

4¼ cups (553 g) all-purpose or bread flour, plus more as needed

1 large egg, lightly beaten

Grease two cookie sheets with butter. Arrange the balls on the cookie sheets, 6 balls per sheet. Cover with a dish towel and let rise until puffy, 30 minutes.

Preheat the oven to 400°F.

Bake the buns for 10 to 12 minutes, until golden brown.

And now for your next recipe . . .

These buns are just the right size for the black-eyed pea and mushroom burgers (page 199). If you do double the batch, freeze the extra buns unsliced in a cloth produce bag. When you crave burgers again, you'll have buns ready.

Homemade Chili Powder

You may have many of the ingredients to make this potent chili powder on hand, such as cumin seeds, garlic granules, dried oregano, and smoked paprika. This recipe also calls for dried hot peppers. Look for them in bulk stores and Mexican markets.

Ancho peppers, like their fresh counterpart, poblano peppers, impart a mild heat and rich flavor to food; and in this spice blend, they help balance out the very hot chile de árbol. You can also use guajillo peppers, which fall somewhere between the two on the heat scale.

Add your chili powder to the black-eyed pea and mushroom burgers (page 199) or season the chili (page 222). It also makes a delicious seasoning for the roasted chickpeas (page 240).

Turn on the overhead fan, if you have one, to avoid breathing in the fumes as you toast the hot peppers.

With kitchen scissors, snip off the tops of the peppers. Remove the seeds by shaking them out. Snip off 1-inch pieces of the peppers.

Heat a dry, well-seasoned cast-iron pan over medium-high heat. Place the peppers in the pan. Stir and toast for a couple of minutes.

Add the cumin and coriander and continue to stir the pan until the cumin seeds begin to pop, about 2 minutes.

Transfer the contents of the pan to a food processor or high-speed blender; add the garlic, oregano, and paprika and blend well. Do not remove the lid of the food processor or blender until the contents have settled, about 5 minutes. You don't want to inhale the chili powder or get it in your eyes.

Transfer to a jar and store it with your other spices.

Makes ½ cup

3 dried ancho peppers

3 dried chiles de árbol

1 tablespoon cumin seeds

½ teaspoon coriander seeds

1 tablespoon granulated garlic

1½ teaspoons dried Mexican oregano (or marjoram)

½ teaspoon paprika

SYS (Save Your Scraps)

Stash the hot pepper tops to add some heat to your homemade vegetable broth (page 135). You need only a small amount of chiles de árbol to spice up your broth, so use it sparingly.

Apple Scrap Vinegar

Scrap vinegar requires little effort, costs nothing, and brews a generous amount of very strong vinegar. I usually make it just with apple scraps or with apple scraps and a few pear scraps. Pineapple scraps work extremely well (see page 258).

If you always eat your apple peels—and bravo for preventing food waste—save any cores and apple bits in the freezer until you have amassed a pile large enough to brew a batch of this. Freezing temperatures won't harm the microbes that ferment this. They'll simply take a nap.

Ordinarily, when you ferment anything alcoholic, you want to prevent an invasion of *Acetobacter* bacteria, which turn alcohol into vinegar. Here, you want to attract this bacterium. To achieve this, brew the scrap vinegar in a wide-mouth jar to increase the surface area that comes into contact with the air. Cover it securely with tightly woven but breathable thin fabric, such as cotton.

When the vinegar tastes, well, vinegary, use it for cooking, cleaning, and after diluting with water, rinsing your hair after washing it with a shampoo bar or a small amount of either baking soda or rye flour. I have even made a beautiful wood stain with my scrap vinegar by adding steel wool to a jar of it and letting it sit for several days.

Please don't feel daunted by the long recipe. The process of making scrap vinegar is quite simple: Stuff ingredients into a jar. Stir daily. Wait. Strain. Bottle. Enjoy.

Combine the apple scraps, sugar, and water in a large, clean, wide-mouth glass jar and stir. Place a smaller jar inside the larger jar to push down the scraps and submerge them in the water. Submerging the scraps in the liquid will prevent mold from developing on them. Cover everything securely with a thin cloth to keep out impurities. Keep the jar on the counter at room temperature.

recipe continues »→

Makes about 4 cups

Peels and cores from 8 large apples (about 4 cups)

1 heaping tablespoon granulated, sucanat, rapadura, or coconut sugar

Enough water to just cover the apple scraps (4 to 5 cups)

(Scale these amounts up or down, depending on the quantity of your apple scraps)

Notes

- If your scrap vinegar turns out weak and more yellow than golden, add a spoonful of sugar to feed the microbes, which will then create more acid. They will also create more carbon dioxide, which will create pressure in a closed jar, so be sure to open the jar every day or two to release this pressure.

- Kahm yeast is a common problem when brewing scrap vinegar. This harmless white film can form on the top of the liquid. Skim off as much as you can. For more on kahm yeast, see page 38.

- Whitish sediment may settle on the bottom of the jar. To remove, strain the vinegar through a tightly woven cloth into a clean jar, leaving as much sediment behind as possible.

← recipe continued from previous page

Over the next several days, stir your scraps several times a day when you think of it. Stirring aerates your ferment, encouraging microbial activity and helping to prevent mold or kahm yeast from forming on the surface. I drink too much tea, and stir my scrap vinegar every time I go into the kitchen to brew another cup.

After a few days, your concoction should start to bubble. At this point, you can stir less often—once a day. After several days of bubbling, the contents of the jar will start to smell slightly alcoholic. Fermentation times vary, but your vinegar will likely begin to taste sour after about another week.

Strain out the fruit after the bubbling has subsided (10 days to 2 weeks from when you began). The fruit will no longer taste sweet. Compost the spent scraps. If you detect zero carbonation, pour the vinegar into a clean bottle. Otherwise, return it to the jar until you see no evidence of bubbling. After bottling, to be safe, open your bottle after a couple of weeks to release any carbon dioxide that may have built up inside.

Brewed properly, this vinegar keeps indefinitely in the cupboard.

And now for your next recipe . . .

If a jellyfish-like primordial blob forms in your vinegar, congratulations! After reading in Sandor Katz's book *The Art of Fermentation* that vinegar SCOBYs (symbiotic culture of bacteria and yeast) have a similar composition to kombucha SCOBYs, I began to successfully brew kombucha with my scrap vinegar SCOBYs. If you'd like to brew kombucha but have been unable to find a SCOBY, you might be able to grow one this way. But be patient! *If* the SCOBY forms, it may take several weeks.

YOU CAN MAKE THAT? STAPLES AND SCRAPS ○ ● THE ZERO-WASTE CHEF

Start with a Sourdough Starter

Sourdough starter, or wild yeast, makes bread rise. Like a pet, it needs regular feedings. Sourdough Protective Services won't appear on your doorstep if you neglect your starter, but you will have to make a new one if you allow yours to languish beyond resuscitation.

With all these regular feedings, the *unfed* starter—the *discard* that you remove from your starter—can pile up quickly, especially if you keep a large starter. For this reason, I keep my starter, Eleanor, small. She's the chihuahua of starters rather than the English mastiff. (And yes, she has a name. And birthday parties. And prefers the pronoun *she*.)

When you bake with your fed, *active* starter, avoid putting all of it into one recipe! Just as you need money to make money, you need starter to make starter. However, if you do accidentally eat all of your starter, you can return to these instructions and start over, pulling your starter up by its bootstraps into a self-made loaf.

To start the starter, combine the rye flour, all-purpose flour, and water in a glass jar or non-reactive bowl (see page 58 regarding bowl choice), using a fork. The starter will have the consistency of very thick batter. Cover tightly with a cloth, plate, or lid. Set in a warm but not hot spot.

Stir daily. If a dry crust forms on top, scrape that off and compost it. After a few days, you will likely see some bubbles in your container. Your starter will also develop an aroma, which may not be completely pleasant. This is normal. When you detect bubbles and the starter's aroma has changed from floury to acidic or yeasty or fruity, or even smells a bit like dirty socks, begin to feed it daily. Until then, continue to stir daily and try to be patient. (New starter parents often feed their starters too soon and remove the nascent bacteria and yeasts, preventing the starter from gestating.)

To feed your starter, stir it down and transfer all but 1 heaping tablespoon of it to a second clean glass jar or dish. Set this aside and put it out of your mind. This is the unfed starter, the *discard*. Store

recipe continues »→

Makes scant ½ cup starter

To Start the Starter

3 tablespoons (25 g) rye or whole wheat flour

3 tablespoons (25 g) all-purpose flour

Generous 3 tablespoons (50 g) room-temperature water

For Each Feeding

Generous 1 tablespoon (22 g) starter

3 tablespoons (25 g) rye or whole-wheat flour

3 tablespoons (25 g) all-purpose flour

Generous 3 tablespoons (50 g) room-temperature water

←« recipe continued from previous page

this second jar in the refrigerator. You'll continue to add discard to it. After about a week of feedings, the accumulated discard will have soured. Use this to bake something, such as pancakes (page 152) or crackers (page 235). Do not use this discard to bake bread. It does not contain enough yeast to make bread rise.

The bowl or jar you started with now has approximately 1 heaping tablespoon of starter remaining. Stir in its feeding of rye flour, all-purpose flour, and water. Cover with a lid and set aside undisturbed until you feed it the next day around the same time.

Continue to feed your starter daily as described, removing a generous 6 tablespoons (about 80 percent) and adding 3 tablespoons (25 g) each of the flours and a generous 3 tablespoons (50 g) water. After its first feedings, the starter will grow a small amount in volume within several hours. After about 1 week of daily feedings, it should double in size within perhaps 4 to 6 hours after every feeding, before slowly falling back down. At this point, your starter has matured. Congratulations, your starter can now bake bread. Think of a cute name.

Notes

- If you want a break from daily feedings once you've established a *mature* starter, store it in the refrigerator and remove it about once a week to feed it. Let it rise for 1 hour or more before returning it to the refrigerator if you don't feel like baking. But do not store your starter in the refrigerator until after you have established it!

- To speed up the feedings, combine equal parts rye flour (or whole wheat) and all-purpose flour in a container. That way, you'll have to measure out only ¾ cup (50 g) of the mixture rather than each of the flours separately.

- If you run out of all-purpose flour, feed your starter 100 percent rye, whole wheat, spelt, or a combination of flours.

- To speed up the rising time a little bit, feed your starter warm—but not hot—water, around 80°F.

- This is a 100 percent hydration starter, meaning it contains equal parts flour and water by weight.

No-Fear Pastry

Flaky, tender pastry is an essential component of zero-waste cook-ing. We all do what we must. Embellish this blank canvas with a variety of ingredients you have on hand. Fill a galette (page 267) with rhubarb or fresh blueberries or juicy peaches in the summer, or a pie shell with tart apples or sweet persimmons or pumpkin custard in the fall. Tuck small amounts of sautéed mushrooms and caramelized onions and roasted butternut squash into a hand pie (see empamosas, page 184). Or drape a sheet of pastry over creamy, vegetable-packed pot pie filling on a cold winter's night (see Gran-ny's Pot Pie, page 220).

Terrified of pastry? Chill! For best results, begin with cold ingredients. Cut up the cold butter and stash it in the refrigerator before using. Put the flour in there, too, if desired. Chill your tools while you're at it. After you make the dough, chill that. After rolling and filling it, chill it again. Solidified fat in cold dough releases steam in the oven, creating a flaky crust that holds its shape.

For vegan pastry, use coconut oil in place of the butter. Measure out the coconut oil and chill it. If it becomes too solid to work with, let it sit for a few minutes before cutting it into the flour.

If using a food processor, pulse the flour and salt a few times until combined. Add the butter in bits and pulse until the mixture resembles large peas. If making the pastry by hand, whisk the flour and salt together in a bowl and then cut in the butter with either a pastry blender or two knives.

Slowly add the ice water, 1 tablespoon at a time. In the food processor, pulse a few times; by hand, mix with a fork. Continue adding water 1 tablespoon at a time until the dough easily sticks together when you pinch a large piece. If it crumbles, add more ice water but not so much that the dough becomes sticky.

Turn the dough out onto a lightly floured work surface and form into a ball. Flatten into a disk. Place the disk on a plate and invert another plate over it. Chill the dough for at least 1 hour in the refrigerator or 20 minutes in the freezer.

Makes one 9- to 10-inch pie or galette crust

1¼ cups (163 g) all-purpose flour

½ teaspoon salt

½ cup or 1 stick (114 g) unsalted butter or coconut oil, chilled and cut into small pieces

3 to 4 tablespoons (45 to 60 ml) ice water

SYS (Save Your Scraps)

Form a ball with the leftover pastry scraps, roll the ball out into a rectangle, sprinkle with cinnamon and sugar, then roll up into a log and cut into slices with a sharp knife. Bake the slices on a baking sheet at 375°F until golden.

Tender and Tangy Sourdough Tortillas

Americans spend $4 billion yearly on tortillas. Yes, billion with a "b," as in "Bezos." The plastic that packages every one of those tortillas provides some real estate to display the list of sesquipedalian, lab-created additives you may want to avoid consuming. The transparent plastic provides, well, room for transparency.

The good news is that you can easily make tortillas at home that require zero packaging, unless you (a) love the flavor of these so much that you (b) go into business making them, enticed by that $4 billion market. You'll come up with a solution to the packaging.

Once you have prepared and fermented this dough, store it in the refrigerator for up to 5 days if you won't cook the tortillas immediately. When you crave some, tear off a few hunks of dough, roll them out while the pan heats, and enjoy your tortillas in mere minutes.

Because you use unfed sour starter for these, the tortillas have a natural, slightly tangy flavor that goes well with savory dishes. Serve them with the refried beans (page 180) and the huevos rancheros (page 161), or cut them up to dip into the hummus (page 248).

Whisk together the all-purpose flour, whole wheat flour, and salt in a medium, non-reactive bowl (see page 58).

Cut the coconut oil or butter into the flour mixture with a pastry blender, two knives, or your fingers until crumbly.

Add the starter and about half the water. Mix to make a stiff dough. If it's too stiff, add the remaining water. The dough should be quite sticky. With your hand, incorporate any remaining flour that you are unable to mix into the dough.

Makes ten 6-inch tortillas

1½ cups (195 g) all-purpose flour, plus more as needed

¼ cup (34 g) whole wheat flour

½ teaspoon salt

3 tablespoons (43 g) solid coconut oil or unsalted butter

½ cup (140 g) sourdough starter discard (see page 105), stirred down

⅓ cup (80 g) water or whey leftover from making ricotta (see page 117)

Knead the dough in the bowl for 2 to 3 minutes until smooth. Cover the bowl with a plate and ferment the dough on the counter up to 10 hours (see Note). Store in the refrigerator for up to 5 days if you won't cook immediately after fermenting. When ready to use, let the dough sit at room temperature for 15 minutes to make rolling easier.

Place the dough on a generously floured work surface. Cut into 10 pieces, roll into balls, and flatten. Dust the top of one piece lightly with flour. With a rolling pin, roll it out into a 6-inch circle, a scant ⅛ inch thick. Continue rolling out the tortillas, adding more flour to the dough and work surface as you work.

Heat a dry, well-seasoned cast-iron skillet over medium-high heat. Place a tortilla in the hot pan. After 30 to 60 seconds, when air bubbles have formed on top of the tortilla, flip it and cook for about another 30 seconds on the other side. Transfer to a towel-lined bowl and fold the towel over the top to keep the tortilla warm and soft.

Continue to cook the tortillas, transferring them to the bowl. Serve the softest tortillas, on the bottom of the basket, first.

Reheat and soften any leftover tortillas by warming them for 20 to 30 seconds each in a hot skillet. You can also place them in a steamer basket over a pot of simmering water.

Notes

- You can also make the dough in a food processor, similar to how you make pastry. Pulse the flours and salt, add the coconut oil, and pulse until crumbly. Add the unfed starter and about half the water, and pulse just until combined. Add as much of the remaining water as necessary and pulse until you have a stiff, sticky dough.

- If desired, skip the fermentation and proceed to make the tortillas immediately after making the dough.

And now for your next recipe . . .

Make baked tortilla chips with any leftover tortillas. Brush both sides of each leftover tortilla with olive oil. With kitchen scissors, cut each tortilla into 8 triangles. Arrange on baking sheets, sprinkle with salt, and bake at 350°F for about 10 minutes or until crispy and slightly browned.

Bourbon Street Vanilla Extract

As with many of the foods I make today—kimchi, vegetable scrap broth, sour cream, scrap vinegar, and so on—the first time I made this vanilla extract, I scratched my head and wondered why I hadn't always made this. *It is so easy.* You combine two ingredients in a jar, set the jar aside, shake it occasionally when you remember to, and wait at least two months.

From the money you'll save, to the packaging you'll keep out of the landfill, to the taste, to the small act of resistance curing your own vanilla represents, this is worth the wait. Once it cures, prepare another batch well before the vanilla runs out. You don't want to start more only *after* you've used the last drop unless you bake only twice a year—in which case, I think you should go look at the picture of my Grown-Up Brownies on page 263.

Split the vanilla beans, but don't cut them all the way to the ends.

Place the beans in a jar, pour the bourbon over them, and seal the jar. Shake the jar once a week or whenever you think of it. Make sure to submerge the beans after shaking if they rise above the surface of the liquid.

Allow the vanilla to cure for 2 to 3 months at room temperature before using.

When you make a new batch, either add the spent beans from this batch, or make a second infusion with them. Because the first infusion extracted so much of the vanilla essence, if you start a second infusion, use half as much bourbon to increase the vanilla concentration. This second infusion will take at least 1 month longer to cure than the first batch.

Makes 1 cup

3 vanilla pods, fresh and supple

1 cup bourbon (see Note)

Note

You can also use vodka, rum, brandy, or single malt whiskey in place of bourbon.

And now for your next recipe . . .

After you've cured the vanilla extract with your beans a couple of times, make vanilla-infused sugar. Place the spent beans in a small baking dish and dehydrate in the oven at 200°F for 20 minutes or until dried out. Grind the beans in a clean spice or coffee grinder. Mix the resulting teaspoon or so of ground vanilla into 2 cups of granulated sugar and use it for baking. Or add the sugar to the spice grinder and continue to grind for a superfine vanilla sugar that's similar to confectioners' sugar.

No-Waste Nut and Seed Milk

For the longest time, I really wanted to make nut milk, but I couldn't bring myself to do it. The flavor wasn't the issue—it tastes rich and creamy and is far superior to store-bought nut milk. The problem was the leftover pulp. On the one hand, I couldn't waste it, but on the other hand, how could I transform the bland pulp from something that I felt I *should* eat to something that I actually *wanted* to eat? I *do* want to eat granola (page 158) and I *do* want to eat fruit crumble (page 268), so I add some of the strained pulp to those. You can also add a bit of pulp to soups and stews to thicken them. Once you make up your mind to use all the food, it becomes a game—you become very creative and your meals become extra delicious.

Make your milk with a combination of nuts and seeds and if you'd like to flavor it, stir in vanilla or almond extract and sweetener such as sugar, maple syrup, honey, brown rice syrup, and so on.

Place the nuts or seeds in a jar and cover with water by a couple of inches. Place the lid on the jar and set the jar aside on the counter at room temperature overnight. Or place the jar in the refrigerator for up to 48 hours. The longer the soak, the creamier the milk.

Strain the nuts or seeds and rinse them very well. Place the nuts or seeds and 3 cups fresh water in a standard or high-speed blender and blend for a few minutes, or until the nuts are very finely ground and cannot be broken down further.

Over a large bowl, place a sieve or colander lined with a fine-mesh cloth, such as thin linen, butter muslin, or high-quality, tightly woven cheesecloth. Pour the mixture through the cloth. Let the straining pulp sit for about 10 minutes to allow gravity to remove most of the liquid. Gather up the edges of the cloth to form a ball of pulp and turn and squeeze out as much milk as you can. Or if you prefer, use a nut milk bag to strain the milk.

Makes about 3 cups

1 cup raw, unsalted nuts or raw shelled seeds, such as cashews, almonds, pecans, walnuts, pumpkin seeds, sunflower seeds, or a combination

3 cups water, plus more for soaking

Pinch of salt (optional)

You likely have lots of leftover pulp, which you can use to make a second batch of nut milk. Return the pulp to the blender, add less water than you did for the first batch (about 2 cups), and repeat the process. This batch won't taste as rich and creamy as the first batch. Repeat a third time, if desired. Combine the batches, if desired.

Store the nut or seed milk in a glass jar in the refrigerator for about 5 days. If sediment separates from the liquid in the refrigerator, shake the jar before serving. If you don't want to use the pulp right away, freeze it.

Notes

- If you want to sweeten this with a pitted date or two, purée the date(s) along with the almonds so you can strain out any date pulp.

- Nuts contain phytic acid, an anti-nutrient that bonds to minerals, preventing your body from absorbing these minerals. Soaking the nuts in water breaks these bonds, making the nuts and nut milk more digestible. Because the soaking water left over contains these anti-nutrients, do not consume it. Pour the soaking water onto your plants instead.

And now for your next recipe . . .

If desired, dehydrate the pulp in the oven on low heat. Spread it in a thin layer on a baking sheet and dry in the oven at about 225°F for 2 hours, or until completely dried. During dehydration, stir the pulp every 30 minutes or so to break up lumps and prevent it from sticking to the baking sheet. Run the dried pulp through a food processor. Store in the refrigerator or in the freezer. Toss a couple of spoonfuls into pancakes (see page 152), quick bread (see page 157), or crackers (see page 244).

Luscious Cultured Buttermilk

This recipe literally takes all of two minutes to prepare—five, if you spill milk on the counter and stop to wipe it up. You will need a bit of cultured buttermilk to make more buttermilk, so you'll have to buy a small carton of it to get it started. Look for buttermilk that contains cultured milk, and avoid fillers like carrageenan. You can theoretically keep your buttermilk going forever and bequeath it in your will. Choose someone responsible.

Even if you never straight-drink this rich probiotic buttermilk—but, of course, you may want to!—if you regularly buy sour cream or crème fraîche, you'll want some cultured buttermilk on hand so you can make delicious homemade versions of those yourself (see page 118).

Pour the buttermilk and milk into a jar and stir or close with a lid and shake to combine.

Place the jar in a warm, draft-free spot. Wait 24 hours. Transfer the jar to the refrigerator.

The buttermilk will keep for at least 2 weeks. To keep the culture alive, make a fresh batch before eating all of the current batch.

Makes 2 generous cups

¼ cup cultured buttermilk

2 cups whole milk

And now for your next recipe . . .

I know, I know, you're about to flip through the book to find the sour cream recipe so you can eat tastier sour cream and banish those plastic tubs from your life forever (see page 118). The sourdough waffles (page 150) also call for buttermilk. You need 2 cups of buttermilk for those, so culture enough that you have leftover buttermilk to start a new batch.

Yogurt Begets Yogurt

I had been making yogurt since my eldest daughter was a baby but had never stopped to think about what that process entails: fermenting milk. I just knew that if I heated milk and added yogurt from the previous batch (a technique called backslopping), I'd get more yogurt. That's basically all there is to it.

If you let your yogurt strain for two or three days in the refrigerator, you'll render delicious labneh, or yogurt cheese. It tastes something like cream cheese but contains probiotic goodness.

For yogurt-making success, avoid using ultra-pasteurized or ultra-heat-treated (UHT) milk, as those may not ferment well, or even at all. As with many other recipes requiring a starter culture, you'll need to buy yogurt to get started. Look for good-quality yogurt that contains only milk and live cultures.

In a heavy pot, slowly heat the milk to 180°F over medium-low heat, stirring frequently to avoid scalding it. At this temperature, the milk will begin to bubble around the edges of the pot.

Allow the milk to cool to 110°F. It will be warm, not hot.

Stir the yogurt into the milk. Cover the pot with a lid or transfer the liquid to jars or a covered, shallow dish. Put in a warm place overnight. In the morning, transfer the thickened yogurt to the refrigerator.

To make Greek yogurt, strain the yogurt through a coffee filter or sieve lined with cheesecloth or other thin fabric, and place over a container to collect the whey. Set aside for 1 hour or more, until the yogurt has reached your desired consistency.

To make labneh, pour the yogurt into a cloth-lined sieve over a bowl. Place a plate over the sieve and place the bowl in the refrigerator. In a couple of days, after the yogurt has strained to a spreadable consistency, transfer it to a clean jar.

Makes about 3½ cups

4 cups whole milk

½ cup yogurt with live cultures

And now for your next recipe . . .

With the strained probiotic whey, kick-start a ferment such as the ketchup (page 126), add flavor to soup, or make the sourdough tortillas (page 108).

Yes Whey,
You Can Make Ricotta

Very little cheese would go to waste in this world if everyone who eats cheese made cheese at least once in his or her lifetime. When you witness how much milk (a lot) renders how much cheese (a little), you appreciate much more all the resources that went into creating your cheese—the land and water to grow the food to feed the cow to make the milk to make your cheese. You won't allow any to go to waste on your watch. And you'll use the whey, too.

For my ricotta, I use non-homogenized milk and cream that I buy in returnable, refillable glass bottles. Homogenized milk will also work. Ultra-pasteurized or ultra-heat-treated (UHT) milk, however, may not curdle at all.

In a heavy-bottomed pot, combine the milk, cream, buttermilk, and salt, if using.

Heat the mixture slowly over medium heat until it reaches between 190°F and 200°F—the temperature it hits just before it boils. It will curdle at this point. Remove from the heat. Wait 10 to 20 minutes for the curds to sink to the bottom of the pot.

Over a large bowl, place a colander or large sieve lined with a thin, fine-mesh cloth such as butter muslin or high-quality, reusable cheesecloth. Carefully pour in the curdled milk mixture. Let the ricotta strain from 15 minutes to a couple of hours, depending on how wet you want it. Transfer it to a glass container and store in the refrigerator for up to 1 week.

Note

If you don't have cultured buttermilk, add 2 tablespoons lemon juice or 2 tablespoons distilled white vinegar *after* heating the milk. It will then begin to curdle.

Makes about
1½ cups ricotta
and 4 cups whey

4 cups whole milk

1 cup heavy cream

1 cup Luscious Cultured Buttermilk (page 114; see Note)

½ teaspoon salt, if desired

And now for your next recipe . . .

This leftover whey is different from yogurt whey, which contains live cultures, so you won't want to use it to ferment anything. But it renders the burger buns (page 96) and the sourdough tortillas (page 108) softer and adds tangy flavor to the ribollita (page 225). Whey also freezes well.

Two-Ingredient Homemade
Sour Cream or Crème Fraîche

Practically every last spoonful of store-bought sour cream sold in the United States comes in a plastic tub. If you love sour cream, requisitioning it becomes one of your first plastic-free dilemmas. Finding a solution is a rite of passage, like a bat mitzvah of low-waste living.

To make sour cream, stir a bit of cultured buttermilk (page 114) into some half-and-half. Wait. Refrigerate. Devour. To make crème fraîche, follow this same technique but with heavy cream instead of half-and-half. Don't even bother to warm up the ingredients. Just stir and wait. Never waste half-and-half or heavy cream again.

Sour Cream

MAKES 1 CUP

Combine 1 tablespoon cultured buttermilk with 1 cup half-and-half (12% fat) in a clean jar and close the jar. Let sit for 24 hours in warm spot. Transfer to the refrigerator to thicken.

Crème Fraîche

MAKES 1 GENEROUS CUP

Combine ¼ cup cultured buttermilk with 1 cup heavy cream (38% fat) in a clean jar and close the jar. Let sit for 24 hours in a warm spot; it will have the consistency of sour cream. Transfer to the refrigerator to thicken.

And now for your next recipe . . .

Serve the sour cream on the side of the huevos rancheros (page 161), the refried beans (page 180), or any spicy dish that could use a dollop of it. A few spoonfuls of crème fraîche taste delicious in the frittata (page 207) or on top of warm pieces of fruit galette (page 267). Or eat it by the spoonful when no one is looking.

A Tomato for All Seasons: Roasted Tomatoes

When people learn that I don't buy packaged food, they often ask, "What do you do about canned tomatoes?" In our first few months of plastic-free living, I also wondered what I would do about canned tomatoes.

Then my boss taught me a little trick that I now use religiously (zero waste becomes like a religion). Near the end of tomato season every fall, when the prices drop, I buy a few 20-pound cases of tomatoes, quarter them, roast them slowly (usually) with smashed garlic, and freeze them.

I prefer small, dry-farmed Early Girl tomatoes, a wildly popular staple of summer and early fall farmers' markets here in Northern California. Farmers withhold water from these tomatoes, causing distress in the plant and resulting in a smaller tomato that is bursting with an intense, sweet flavor. Meaty San Marzanos also work well for roasting. Juicy heirlooms are a bit too juicy.

Quarter the tomatoes or halve if very small. Arrange in single layers on baking sheets. Spread the garlic across the tomatoes, if desired. Slow-cook in the oven at 250°F for 1½ to 2 hours, until softened, sweet, and roasted.

If desired, when cool, run the tomatoes through a food mill to remove the skins. Transfer to jars to freeze (see page 24 for freezing in jars).

Note

If you prefer canning over freezing, process these jarred roasted tomatoes in a hot water bath. Be sure to add extra acid, such as citric acid, for the tomatoes to can properly.

Makes 6 to 8 quarts, depending on tomato variety

20 pounds ripe tomatoes

1 head of garlic, cloves separated and smashed (optional)

And now for your next recipe . . .

Use these tomatoes in the ribollita (page 225); chana masala (page 197); or chili (page 222); or make your own tomato paste (page 122), ketchup (page 126), and quick tomato sauce (page 227). If you remove the skins, dehydrate the skins for the popcorn seasoning (page 247).

Worth-It Tomato Paste

From prepping the tomatoes, to roasting them, to running them through a food mill, to cooking the rendered pulp down to a paste, this recipe requires five or six hours to complete. *It is worth every minute.* One taste of this and you'll wonder (a) just what have you've been eating all these years? and (b) why didn't you buy 40 pounds of tomatoes? And if you've already roasted several pounds of tomatoes (see page 121), you have a head start on this absolutely delicious recipe.

And don't worry; that five or six hours is not hands-on time!

If using ripe tomatoes, place them in a large stockpot with the olive oil and simmer over medium heat until softened and juicy, and the skins begin to separate from the flesh, about 40 minutes.

Attach the disk with small holes to your food mill. In batches, run the tomatoes through the food mill to remove the skins and seeds. Save these for vegetable broth (page 135). (If using roasted tomatoes that still have the skins on them, run them through your food mill.)

Place the tomato purée back in the stockpot. Add the maple syrup, bay leaves, and salt. Gently simmer over medium-low heat until thick, about 1 hour. Stir often to avoid burning. (You could skip this step, but the tomato purée will require much more time in the oven to cook down to a paste.)

Preheat the oven to 250°F and coat two 9 by 13-inch glass baking dishes with some olive oil.

Spread half the tomato purée evenly in each dish and place in the oven.

Check on the tomatoes and stir every 20 minutes for about 2½ to 3 hours, until thick, sticky, and reduced by about half.

Makes 2½ cups

10 pounds ripe tomatoes, quartered, or between 3 and 4 quarts roasted tomatoes (page 121; see Note)

2 tablespoons olive oil, plus more to seal jars, if desired

¼ cup maple syrup

2 bay leaves

1 tablespoon plus ½ teaspoon salt

Note

Plum (San Marzano) tomatoes and Early Girl round tomatoes are good choices for tomato paste. Juicy heirloom tomatoes take much longer to cook down and render less tomato paste.

recipe continues »→

← recipe continued from previous page

After the tomato paste has cooled, fill small jars with it, top with a thin layer of olive oil, and keep in the refrigerator for at least 1 month or in the freezer for several months. Or freeze in ice cube trays (do not top with oil). Once frozen, move the tomato paste cubes to wide-mouth glass jars and take the cubes from the freezer as needed.

And now for your next recipe . . .

Make another holy grail of zero-waste living: ketchup. Now that you've made tomato paste, you've practically made ketchup. Ditch the plastic bottle and corn syrup–filled Heinz and substitute a version you'll actually encourage your kids to eat (page 126).

Stepped-Up Ketchup

When I developed this recipe, I actually intended to add ground cloves. But I accidentally grabbed the jar of garam masala out of my jar-crammed, of-course-I-know-where-everything-is-in-here spice cabinet. What a serendipitous mistake! The resulting ketchup tasted delicious.

If you'd rather eat this immediately or skip the fermentation, omit the whey or brine and store the ketchup in the refrigerator after mixing everything. If you do intend to ferment it, do not use whey strained from ricotta, as it does not contain live cultures. The whey from yogurt or the brine from fermented vegetables, such as the dilly beans (page 175) does. These good microbes give you an extra dose of gut-friendly goodness. Even with french fries.

Mix the tomato paste, kombucha, honey, whey, cinnamon, garam masala, cayenne, and ¼ teaspoon salt (if using) in a jar and close it.

Place the jar on the counter for 3 to 5 days to ferment, depending on the warmth of your kitchen. This bubbles up only slightly, unlike sauerkraut or kimchi, which bubble vigorously. Burp the jar (i.e., open it) daily.

Transfer the jar to the refrigerator. It will keep for several months, but because the ketchup will continue to slowly ferment, it tastes best if eaten within 1 month.

Notes

- Brine from fermented vegetables is very salty. If you use brine, omit the salt when mixing the ingredients. Taste and then add salt, if desired.

- If you don't want to ferment this, omit the whey or brine. Top the ketchup with a thin layer of olive oil and store it in the refrigerator immediately after making it. It will keep for at least 1 month.

- If using apple cider vinegar, choose a brand that contains the vinegar mother, such as Braggs, to help kick-start the ferment. You could also use very strong Apple Scrap Vinegar (page 101).

- This recipe will ferment with store-bought tomato paste. Look for tomato paste that contains only tomatoes.

Makes a scant 3 cups

2 cups Worth-It Tomato Paste (page 121) or store-bought (see Note)

½ cup vinegary kombucha (see page 255) or apple cider vinegar

¼ cup raw honey

2 tablespoons whey from making yogurt (see page 115) or brine from fermented vegetables (see page 175)

⅛ teaspoon ground cinnamon

⅛ teaspoon garam masala

⅛ teaspoon cayenne pepper

¼ teaspoon salt (optional; see Note)

And now for your next recipe . . .

This tastes amazing with the frittata (page 207) or scrambled eggs.

Egg White Aioli

Capulets and Montagues. Democrats and Republicans. Oil and water. These, we are told, never mix. This aioli, however—a creamy, mayonnaise-like garlic sauce made with an egg white (water) and oil—proves that we all really can just get along. Plus it tastes good.

As peacemaker, you'll bring your opposing factions together in less than five minutes. Spread your aioli on sandwiches, fold it into a classic potato salad, or serve it as a dip for a crudité platter. You can make aioli with egg yolks, but I've made it here with an egg white because, if you bake often, you may experience egg separation anxiety—that what-do-I-do-with-this? panic caused by the one lone egg white baking often generates (see Note).

If using an immersion blender, place the egg white, salt, lemon juice, garlic, and oil in a deep wide-mouth jar. Set the immersion blender in the bottom of the jar and whirl the ingredients for less than 1 minute, until combined into a mayonnaise-like sauce.

If using a food processor or blender, purée the egg white, salt, lemon juice, and garlic, scraping down the sides of the processor or blender, if necessary. With the machine running, pour in the oil slowly. The aioli will thicken quickly. As soon as it does, turn off the machine immediately. (If you process it for longer, it can become thick and lumpy, similar to how whipped cream can turn quickly from a creamy to a buttery consistency.)

Store the aioli in a glass jar in the refrigerator for up to 5 days.

Makes about ⅔ cup

1 large egg white

⅛ teaspoon salt

½ teaspoon fresh lemon juice

2 medium garlic cloves, smashed

½ cup avocado or grapeseed oil

Note

If you have an extra egg yolk rather than egg white, make egg yolk aioli.

And now for your next recipe . . .

If you started with a whole egg to make this, and not a leftover egg white, the simplest way to use up that egg yolk is to toss it into some scrambled eggs or add it to the frittata (page 207). You can also add it to the sourdough pancakes (page 152).

As You Like It Honey Mustard

Homemade mustard almost makes itself. However, after it practically makes itself, let it sit for several days before you eat it, as it needs time to mellow. For a few days after you grind the soaked mustard seeds, they taste so hot and bitter that you'll only want to eat your mustard immediately if you need a good cry. But wait a few days and you'll have an epiphany: *You'll never have to buy gourmet mustard again.*

In a small jar, combine the mustard seeds, vinegar, wine, honey, salt, turmeric, and cayenne and mix well. Close the jar and let it sit on the counter at room temperature for 1 to 2 days.

Process the ingredients in a food processor until smooth but with many intact mustard seeds. (If you prefer a smoother consistency, continue processing.)

Transfer the mustard to a jar and let sit at room temperature for 5 days to a week.

Taste and adjust seasonings, if desired. Store in the refrigerator for several months. The flavor will mellow over time.

Makes ½ cup

¼ cup yellow mustard seeds

¼ cup strong Apple Scrap Vinegar (page 101), strong kombucha vinegar (page 255), or apple cider vinegar

¼ cup dry white wine

1 tablespoon raw honey

¾ teaspoon salt, plus more as needed

½ teaspoon ground turmeric

⅛ teaspoon cayenne pepper

And now for your next recipe . . .

Have a mere teaspoon of mustard smeared across the bottom and sides of the jar? Enjoy every last smidgeon by making salad dressing directly in the jar. Try the lemon-garlic dressing for the bean, vegetable, and grain salad (page 206).

Any-Nut Nut Butter

The number of possible flavor combinations for nut butters makes a great math problem.

Joe wants to impress his coffee date, a zero waster, with a jar of homemade nut butter. In his well-stocked kitchen, he has squirreled away jars of peanuts, cashews, pecans, pistachios, and almonds. (How is Joe still single?) The recipe he has chosen from his favorite cookbook—the book that prompted his date to swipe right when she saw him holding it in his profile pic—says he can also flavor homemade nut butter with salt, cinnamon, dried coconut, honey, or dates, or even transform it into Nutella, if desired.

How many different combinations of nut butter can Joe make?

How much longer will Joe be on Tinder?

Show your work.

Preheat the oven to 350°F.

On a rimmed baking sheet, spread the nuts out in a single layer. Toast for 5 minutes. Stir. Toast for up to another 5 minutes, or until golden but not dark.

If using hazelnuts, after the nuts have cooled enough to handle, place them on a towel. Cover them and rub them around inside the towel to remove most of the skins. Don't worry if you can't get all the skins off.

Process the nuts in a food processor. They will transform from crumbly to a large ball to a creamy paste that finally releases oil. Be patient and wait for that final oil-releasing stage. You may have to process the nuts for up to 10 minutes.

Add any add-ins and process as well.

Store at room temperature unless you eat nut butter slowly. For longer-term storage (2 months or longer), keep in the refrigerator.

Makes 1 cup

1½ cups raw, unsalted nuts, such as almonds, cashews, pecans, peanuts, pistachios, walnuts, hazelnuts, or macadamia nuts

¼ teaspoon salt (optional)

Add-ins as desired (such as salt, vanilla extract, honey or maple syrup, dates, cinnamon, cocoa powder, or melted chocolate)

And now for your next recipe . . .

Joe had you at homemade Nutella. To make that, first make hazelnut butter as described here. After it has become very creamy, add the following ingredients and process until smooth and uniform:

¾ cup confectioners' sugar or superfine vanilla sugar (see page 110)

⅜ cup unsweetened cocoa powder

Large pinch of salt

½ teaspoon Bourbon Street Vanilla Extract (page 110) or store-bought

2 to 4 tablespoons melted coconut oil, for desired consistency

This tastes delicious with the sourdough graham crackers (page 244) and really, just about anything.

How to Cook Any Dried Bean

Like many things low waste, cooking with dried beans requires a bit of planning ahead, but not too much. And that planning, as usual, pays off. Beans cooked from their dried form have a creamy, chewy texture; they taste better than canned; they contain only the ingredients that you add to the pot yourself; and they cost little to buy.

Almost every grocery store in America with a bulk section sells unpackaged dried beans. Some of these bulk bins have a faster turnover than others, however. Either way, you may have no idea how fresh your dried beans are. Fresher dried beans cook faster and more evenly than older ones. As dried beans age, they continue to dry out, but they do so unevenly. As they cook, some turn mushy while others remain stubbornly crunchy. For more even cooking, soak the beans in water for at least six hours beforehand. Soaking also speeds up the cooking time (thereby using less energy) and reduces the sugars (oligosaccharides) in the beans that can cause people discomfort and gas.

To save time, since you'll have a pot or slow cooker or pressure cooker bubbling away anyway, you may as well cook extra beans and set them aside for another dish. Cooking more beans requires literally no additional work as long as your pot can accommodate them all and you don't need to cook them in batches. When you need beans for a dish, simply reach into the refrigerator, grab a jar or two of them, and thank your earlier self for having had such excellent foresight. Beans also freeze well.

1 cup dried bean, such as pinto beans, black-eyed peas, chickpeas, kidney beans, borlotti or cranberry beans, adzuki beans, or black beans

Water or Save-Scraps-Save-Cash Vegetable Broth (page 135)

Optional seasonings: bay leaf, garlic, sprigs of rosemary, thyme, oregano, or sage

--------- Soaking ---------

Pick through the beans and discard any debris, such as small pebbles, soil, or twigs. Rinse the beans in a colander under cool running water. Place the rinsed beans in a large bowl and cover with 3 inches of water. Place a large plate over the bowl. Soak the beans for at least 6 hours and up to 14 hours.

Drain and rinse the beans well. (Do not cook with this soaking water, as it contains the indigestible sugars that soaking helps reduce.)

Alternatively, if you don't have time to soak the beans for several hours, do a quick soak. Place the rinsed beans and water in a pot, bring to a boil, turn off the heat, and let the beans sit, covered, for 1 hour. Drain and proceed to cooking.

————————————— Cooking in a Standard Pot —————————————

Place the rinsed beans in a Dutch oven or other heavy pot large enough to hold the beans and enough water or broth to cover them by 2 inches. Add the herbs and garlic, if desired.

Over medium-high heat, bring the beans to a boil and immediately turn down to a simmer. Simmer the beans over low heat, partially covered with a lid, until tender, 1 to 3 hours. (Simmering gently helps render evenly cooked beans that remain intact.) If necessary, replenish the water as the beans cook.

The beans are done when they pass the "5-bean test." If you eat 5 beans and all 5 are tender, then all the beans are cooked. If 1 bean fails the test, continue to cook the beans and check them every 15 minutes.

————————————— Cooking in a Slow Cooker —————————————

If cooking kidney beans, bring them to a boil in a pot of water on the stove and cook for 10 minutes before proceeding to the next step. (Kidney beans contain the toxin phytohemagglutinin, which boiling neutralizes.)

Place the soaked beans in the inner pot of a slow cooker. Add enough water or broth to cover the beans by about 2 inches. Add herbs and garlic, if desired. Cook on low for 5 to 8 hours.

After 5 hours, do the 5-bean test. If 1 bean fails, continue to cook the beans and check them every 15 to 30 minutes.

Storage

Store any beans you won't use immediately in their cooking liquid. They will keep for about 1 week in the refrigerator. They also freeze well; see page 24 for freezing in jars.

recipe continues »→

←« recipe continued from previous page

———————— Cooking in a Pressure Cooker ————————

Place the soaked beans in the pressure cooker. Add enough water or broth to cover the beans by about 2 inches. (Do not fill it with beans and water past the maximum fill line. If necessary, cook the beans in batches.) Add several drops of oil to the water to prevent the vent pipe from clogging. Add the herbs and garlic, if desired.

Slide the lid into place. Bring the pot to pressure over high heat. Depending on your pressure cooker and the type of bean, your beans will cook quickly, in 1 to 10 minutes. (Consult the manual for your model to determine accurate cooking times.)

And now for your next recipe . . .

When draining the beans, save the flavorful broth for a soup, such as ribollita (page 225), or use it in recipes that call for vegetable broth. Store the bean broth in the refrigerator for several days or in the freezer for several months.

Save-Scraps-Save-Cash Vegetable Broth

The last time I bought vegetable broth, my kids were still kids, my hair was free of gray, and Bruno Mars loved me just the way I was. Over my decade sans store-bought broth, I estimate that this homemade scrap broth has saved me at least $250 (10 Tetra Paks of broth/year).

This essentially free scrap broth tastes delicious, contains only the simple ingredients you put into it, squeezes every last drop of goodness out of food scraps you'd planned on composting before you bought this book, and has not been contaminated by the plastic packaging it did not come packaged in.

Think of today as the first day of the rest of your vegetable scrap–collecting life. From this day forward, when you prep vegetables for dinner, lunches, snacks, and so on, you will save:

Yield varies

Vegetable scraps and peels
Water

- Asparagus woody ends
- Bell pepper bits
- Broccoli bits, in moderation
- Carrot ends
- Cauliflower cores, in moderation
- Celery bits and leaves
- Corn kernels, corn cobs, and corn husks
- Cucumber skins
- Eggplant peels, in moderation

- Garlic bits
- Green bean tails
- Herb stems, in moderation
- Hot pepper trimmings, in moderation
- Leek greens and white ends
- Lettuce trimmings
- Mushroom stems
- Onion and shallot trimmings and their skins, in moderation
- Parsnip peelings

- Potato skins, in moderation
- Pumpkin fibers and skins
- Scraps of apples or pear cores, or grapes too
- Spinach trimmings
- Summer or winter squash bits
- Tomato cores and skins
- And so on . . .

Freeze everything until you have amassed enough scraps to make a batch of broth. Because you'll find the bits easier to remove from the jars once they've thawed somewhat, plan ahead a little bit, if possible.

recipe continues »→

← recipe continued from previous page

Place the scraps in a large pot and just barely cover with water. Don't worry if some bits poke through the surface. After simmering, the scraps will soften and shrink down.

Bring to a boil and reduce to low heat. Simmer for 20 to 30 minutes.

Strain the scraps. Place a metal colander lined with a thin cloth or nut milk bag inside a large metal bowl and gently pour in the contents of the pot. After the scraps have cooled enough to handle, gather up the edges of the cloth to form a ball around the scraps. Turn and squeeze out as much broth as you can. Compost the scraps.

Use the broth immediately, store it in the refrigerator, or once it has cooled, freeze in jars or ice cube trays. Once the cubes have frozen, transfer them to glass jars (see page 24 for freezing in jars).

And now for your next recipe . . .

You have so many to choose from! Add your broth to pot pie (page 220) or cauliflower and potato dal (page 217), cook soaked dried beans in it (see page 132), or simply cook grains such as rice or couscous in it.

Lemon or Lime Curd
on Everything

Most curd recipes instruct you to place plastic wrap directly on the surface of your hot curd as it cools in order to prevent a skin from forming on top. Personally, I would rather find that a skin has formed on my cooled curd than to eat food that came into contact with plastic while that food was hot. And here's a little secret: *You can eat this skin and you won't die.* Some people actually *like* this skin. If you don't, peel it off and feed it to someone who does. Or pull a Tom Sawyer: "Well I *guess* you can eat my lemon curd skin. *But just this once.*"

Scrub the lemons or limes well and pat dry. Zest them with a rasp grater or a lemon zester. Whichever method you choose, be careful not to include the very bitter white pith; you'll need 2 teaspoons zest.

Juice the lemons or limes after zesting; you'll need ½ cup juice.

In a heatproof glass or metal bowl, or in the top of a double boiler, whisk together the egg yolks and sugar until smooth. Whisk the juice and zest into the egg yolk–sugar mixture.

Fill a small pot with 2 inches of water and bring to a simmer. Place the bowl on the pot of gently simmering water and whisk constantly for 7 to 10 minutes, until the mixture coats the back of a clean metal spoon.

Wearing oven mitts, remove the hot bowl from the pot immediately.

Whisk in the butter, 1 piece at a time, until fully incorporated. Transfer to a jar and refrigerate, where the curd will thicken as it cools.

Makes 1½ cups

4 lemons or limes

4 large egg yolks

½ cup sugar

6 tablespoons (¾ stick) cold unsalted butter, cut into 6 equal pieces

And now for your next recipe . . .

Don't allow the 4 egg whites left over from this recipes to send you into a panic! Use a couple to make a double batch of the spiced nuts (page 239), whip up some egg white aioli (page 127) in minutes, or freeze your egg whites to use later.

8

Rise Up:
Breakfast
and Breads

#EasyWhenYouKnowHow Sourdough Bread

I became a sourdough disciple while on a quest to make bread with as few ingredients as possible. Rather than buy yeast, I wanted to capture and nurture wild yeast in a mixture of flour and water to create a sourdough starter. Add more flour and water and a bit of salt to the starter and you can create gorgeous, mouth-watering loaves with three basic ingredients, one of which comes out of your tap essentially for free.

On social media, I follow an Irish baker named Joe Fitzmaurice, who once used a hashtag that sums up what I have written here: #EasyWhenYouKnowHow. If the more detailed steps that follow look intimidating, you can lump them together into these mere 7 steps:

1. Make a leaven.
2. Soak the flours.
3. Combine the leaven with the soaked flours.
4. Stretch and fold the dough during the bulk fermentation.
5. Shape the dough.
6. Proof the dough.
7. Bake the bread.

I based this recipe on Michael Pollan's recipe from his book *Cooked: A Natural History of Transformation* and Chad Robertson's in *Tartine Bread*.

If you use 100 percent freshly milled flour that you grind yourself, you will bake very dense loaves. For more airy loaves, use a maximum of about two-thirds freshly ground and one-third store-bought flour—if you decide to grind your own flour, which is not necessary.

As you prepare your bread, take lots of notes, paying attention to the smell, feel, and taste of the dough at its various stages. These all serve as clues to the dough's progress. I've presented a rough schedule for making the bread; adjust these times to fit your plans.

recipe continues »→

Makes 2 loaves

Recommended Equipment
Using the proper equipment yields better results. If you decide you want to bake sourdough bread regularly, I highly recommend acquiring the following tools (see page 56 for more information on these and for alternatives).

Kitchen scale

Dutch oven

Dough scraper

Razor blade or lame

Banneton baskets

For the Leaven
⅜ cup (50 g) rye flour

⅜ cup (50 g) all-purpose flour

Scant ½ cup (100 g) warm water, about 80°F

1 tablespoon (17 g) active sourdough starter (page 105)

For the Dough
4½ cups (600 g) whole wheat flour

2 cups (225 g) rye flour

1½ cups (175 g) all-purpose flour

3 cups plus 2 tablespoons (750 ml) warm water, about 80°F

1½ tablespoons (25 g) coarse salt

Generous 3 tablespoons (50 g) warm water, for dissolving salt

← recipe continued from previous page

Also keep in mind that your dough will ferment more quickly or more slowly depending on your kitchen environment—the heat, humidity, and resident microbes.

———————————— Day 1 ∘ 9 p.m. ————————————

Begin with an active sourdough starter (see page 105). That is, before I make my leaven, I will have fed my starter earlier in the day, at 6 a.m. and then again at 2 p.m. (I prefer to feed it twice, but sometimes I will have fed it only once during the day.) The leaven is essentially a larger starter that you make specifically for your recipe.

1. In a non-reactive medium bowl, make the leaven. Combine the flours, warm water, and fed sourdough starter. Cover with a plate to prevent a crust from forming on top and place the leaven in a warm but not hot spot.

2. Soak the flours for the dough. In a large non-reactive bowl, combine the flours and warm water. Use your hand to incorporate everything well. Cover tightly with a plate and set aside at room temperature.

———————————— Day 2 ∘ 7 a.m. ————————————

1. Combine the leaven with the soaked flours, using a clean, wet hand. Let rest for 20 minutes. Meanwhile, combine the salt and warm water.

2. Add the salt water to the flour mixture and thoroughly mix with your hand. Note the time. This is the beginning of the bulk fermentation. Let rest for 20 minutes.

3. Stretch and fold the dough for the first time. Wet your hand, reach underneath the bottom of the dough, pull the dough up, and fold it over onto itself. Turn the bowl a quarter turn and repeat the stretching and folding. Repeat 2 more times, stretching and folding for a total of 4 times.

recipe continues ⟩→

←« recipe continued from previous page

4. Do these sets of stretches and folds every 30 minutes or so for the first hour. As the dough develops more air, handle it less. After a couple sets of folds, wait 40 minutes before the next set, then wait 45 minutes for the remaining sets of stretches and folds. (Don't worry if you forget to do one of these sets; the dough is very forgiving.) Depending on the heat and humidity of your kitchen, you end the bulk fermentation after 4 or 5 hours. My dough begins to break down around 5 hours, so I do not go past 4½ hours. Your bulk fermentation may require more or less time. The dough will be airy and billowy at the end of the bulk fermentation.

Add-Ins

If you want to add seeds, nuts, olives, or raisins to your sourdough bread, do so immediately *after* the second set of stretches and folds of the dough. Squeeze the add-ins through the dough with your fingers.

- **Seeds:** A combination of sesame, sunflower, and flax seeds with a small amount of fennel seeds is a good choice. Use 1½ cups (220 g) total. Toast for 10 minutes in the oven at 350°F. Then soak the seeds in about 1 cup warm water for 30 minutes before adding to the dough. The seeds will absorb most of the water; strain off any remaining water.

- **Nuts:** Toast 1½ cups (192 g) at 350°F for 5 to 10 minutes, until fragrant but not dark. Chop large, whole nuts into smaller pieces.

- **Olives:** Chop 3 cups (400 g) whole pitted olives into smaller pieces.

- **Raisins:** Soak 3 cups (400 g) golden raisins in warm water for 30 minutes, then strain before adding to the dough.

1. Lightly flour a wooden board. Turn out your dough onto it and cut the dough in half with your dough scraper. With your wet hands, rotate each half gently while pushing the sides toward the bottom until you have 2 fairly uniform rounds of dough. Don't overwork the dough.

2. Cover each with a towel and let rest 20 minutes. Meanwhile, sprinkle the banneton baskets generously with flour. (If you don't have banneton baskets, line 2 bowls with cloth and generously flour the cloth.)

3. Because you want the dough to stick to itself as you fold it, do not add more flour to the dough or work surface unless necessary. With your dough scraper, flip the first round of dough over. Wet your hands and pull gently on the top and sides of the dough to form an 8-inch square. Fold the square like a letter, in three sections, folding the left side onto the middle and then the right side over that. You've now got a rectangle. Starting at the bottom, roll up the dough into a taut loaf. Avoid squeezing out the air bubbles as you work. Dust the top of the dough with flour. Repeat with the other dough piece.

4. Place the loaves in the baskets, with the seam sides up. (When you later drop the loaves into the Dutch oven, the seam sides will face down.) Cover the loaves with a cloth. (If you don't have a Dutch oven and will instead bake in a loaf pan, use that to proof the dough as well. Sprinkle the loaf pan generously with cornmeal before adding the dough to it.)

5. Proof the loaves, either overnight in the refrigerator or for 2 to 3 hours at room temperature (and bake the same day). I get much better results from an overnight cold proof in the refrigerator for between 8 and 16 hours.

recipe continues »→

←« recipe continued from previous page

———————————————— Day 3 • 6 a.m. ————————————

If you've done a cold proof, remove the first loaf from the refrigerator.

1. Place the Dutch oven (with lid) in the oven and preheat to 500°F. (Alternatively, heat a pizza stone.) When the oven is hot, remove the Dutch oven from the oven and remove the lid. Hold one basket of dough above the pot and drop the loaf into the pot, being very careful not to burn yourself. (Alternatively, drop the dough from the basket onto the baking stone or onto a baking sheet sprinkled with cornmeal.)

2. Score the loaf using a lame or a very sharp knife. Dig deeply into the dough with the lame, making either a single line, an *X*, a hashtag, or other simple design. Wearing your oven mitts, put the lid back on the Dutch oven and return the pot to the oven. (Or, score the loaf on the baking stone or baking sheet.)

3. Reduce the oven temperature to 450°F. Bake for 20 minutes.

4. Remove the lid from the Dutch oven. You will now discover whether your dough has risen nicely while baking. Bake another 20 to 23 minutes without the lid, until the crust has browned and caramelized. (If you've baked in a loaf pan or on a pizza stone or baking sheet, check for doneness a few minutes early.)

5. Tip the baked loaf out of the Dutch oven and cool on a cooling rack. (If using the pizza stone or baking sheet, transfer the baked loaf to the cooling rack.) Let the bread cool. Resist the temptation to tear into it right away. The bread continues to bake after you remove it from the oven.

6. Pull the second loaf from refrigerator. Place the Dutch oven back in the oven. Heat the oven to 500°F for 15 minutes. Repeat steps 12 through 16.

Store the loaves in a cloth produce bag, if desired. If you'd like to freeze your bread without plastic, store it whole in a cloth produce bag for up to 2 weeks.

Whole Wheat Sourdough Buttermilk Waffles

If your family cannot let go of those store-bought frozen waffles in the yellow box, make a batch of these. You'll wish convincing people to do your bidding was always so easy. Like most things zero waste, these waffles do require a bit of planning ahead, but not much. You'll need to make the sponge the night before you make the waffles. Think of this delayed gratification not as a hardship but, rather, as getting a head start on making the best waffles you've ever tasted.

The night before you make your waffles make the sponge: Mix the starter, buttermilk, and flour in a non-reactive medium bowl. Cover with a plate and set aside overnight at room temperature. In the morning, you should see lots of bubbles in the sponge.

Make the batter: In a small bowl, whisk together the eggs, melted butter, and vanilla. Stir into the sponge, then add the salt and baking soda. Wait a few minutes for the batter to puff up.

Heat a waffle iron and follow the manufacturer's instructions for making the waffles, using about ½ cup batter for each.

Note

If you have neither buttermilk nor yogurt on hand, place 2 tablespoons lemon juice or vinegar in a 2-cup measure. Add enough milk to fill, then stir gently. Let the mixture sit for several minutes, until the milk curdles.

Makes ten 6-inch waffles

For the Sponge

1 cup sourdough starter discard (see page 105), stirred down

2 cups Luscious Cultured Buttermilk (page 114), or 1½ cups Yogurt Begets Yogurt (page 115) plus ½ cup whole milk

2 cups whole wheat flour or a blend of whole wheat and spelt flours

For the Batter

2 large eggs

¼ cup (½ stick) unsalted butter or coconut oil, melted

1 teaspoon Bourbon Street Vanilla Extract (page 110) or store-bought

1 teaspoon salt

1 teaspoon baking soda

And now for your next recipe . . .

These waffles freeze well. Use a cloth bag and freeze for up to 1 week. Thaw them to make sandwiches with nut butter (page 130) or leftover frittata (page 207).

Sweet or Savory
Sourdough Pancakes

As you continue on your sourdough baking adventure, expect this page to become quite dog-eared.

When you feed a starter regularly, you can quickly accumulate a couple jars' worth of unfed sourdough starter in the refrigerator that you obviously don't want to throw out because, well, you're thumbing through a book about zero-waste living. But what can you *do* with all that extra unfed starter encroaching on the other jars that you now use for all the food storage in your refrigerator?

While not lively enough to bake bread, unfed discard does work well in many other recipes that I've included in this book, such as these pancakes, which practically make themselves and use up lots of unfed sourdough starter in one fell swoop. Like crepes, they taste equally delicious topped with sweet or savory toppings. Bonus: You can easily veganize this recipe by omitting the eggs and adding almond meal.

In a medium bowl, combine the starter and, if using, the flour, then whisk in the eggs.

Melt the butter in a large skillet over medium heat and swirl it around to coat the pan. Pour most of the butter into the batter. Stir in the salt and baking soda. Wait a couple of minutes for the batter to puff up a bit.

For each pancake, pour about ½ cup batter into the skillet. Flip the pancakes after bubbles have formed around the edges, about 3 to 4 minutes, then continue to cook for 1 to 2 minutes, until golden brown. Transfer to a plate and keep warm, then continue to cook the pancakes. If the pan looks dry, add more butter as necessary.

Top the pancakes as desired.

Makes four 6-inch pancakes

1 cup sourdough starter discard (see page 105), stirred down

2 heaping tablespoons flour of any kind (optional, for fluffier pancakes; see Note) or almond meal for vegan pancakes

2 large eggs (omit for vegan)

2 tablespoons unsalted butter or coconut oil

¼ teaspoon salt

¼ teaspoon baking soda

And now for your next recipe . . .

Avert food waste on two fronts! Top these pancakes, made from discarded starter you saved, with a quick berry sauce (page 153), cooked with berries past their prime.

Notes

• If you've saved the pulp rendered from making nut milk (see page 112), add this instead of the flour for fluffy pancakes, if desired. Use either wet or dry pulp.

• Lemon zest is another scrappy addition. Add it before the salt and baking soda.

Quick Any-Berry Pancake and Waffle Sauce

Sometimes you may find yourself with more perishable sweet berries on your hands than you can eat quickly, but not enough to make and can jam. So, make this quick berry sauce instead. Store it in the refrigerator for a couple of weeks—if it lasts that long—and use it to top the sourdough pancakes (page 152) or the sourdough waffles (page 150).

The directions call for strawberries, but you can use other fruit, such as raspberries, blueberries, peaches, or even apples. If desired, add a splash of alcohol to the fruit not only to help preserve the sauce but also to brighten the flavor. Grand Marnier goes well with berries, bourbon with peaches, and brandy with apples. As the fruit cooks, most of the alcohol will burn off.

In a medium saucepan, toss together the strawberries, sugar, lemon zest and juice, and alcohol (if using). Place over high heat and bring to a boil, then reduce the heat to medium and simmer for about 10 minutes, mashing the fruit with a potato masher or fork. Cook until the sugar has dissolved and the fruit has cooked down.

Store in a clean jar in the refrigerator for up to 2 weeks.

Makes about 1 cup

1 pound fresh strawberries, hulled, cut in half or quartered if large

¼ cup sugar

Zest and juice of ½ lemon

Splash of Grand Marnier, bourbon, or brandy (optional)

And now for your next recipe . . .

Love fruit-bottom yogurt but not the plastic tubs? Make your own. Place a spoonful of berry sauce in a small jar—a small glass yogurt jar happens to be the perfect size!—and top with yogurt (page 115).

Sourdough Sticky Buns

Every time I pull a tray of these sweet, soft, sticky buns out of the oven, I feel so grateful for what flour and water can do. This dough contains no baker's yeast, yet it puffs up into billowy soft swirls with only sourdough starter—mere flour and water—as the leavening agent. I hope this feat never fails to amaze me.

You'll want to make these buns on special occasions, like the weekend. Curl up in your favorite chair with a good book, a hot cup of tea, one of these buns, and perhaps a purring cat on your lap. Be sure to thank your other pet—your sourdough starter—for its dedication.

—————— Day 1 • 8 p.m. ——————

The night before you make your sticky buns, make the leaven. Combine the flours, water, and starter in a jar or non-reactive bowl, mix well, cover with a lid or plate, and set aside overnight at room temperature.

—————— Day 2 • 6 a.m. ——————

1. Stir down the leaven to remove the bubbles.

2. Make the dough: In a small pot over medium heat, heat the milk just until bubbles form around the edges. Remove from the heat and add the butter and sugar. Stir to melt the butter and combine the ingredients. Allow to cool to about 80°F (warm but not hot).

3. In a large, non-reactive bowl, whisk together the flours and salt. Stir in the milk mixture, the eggs, and the leaven. Finish mixing with your hands to incorporate everything into a sticky, shaggy dough. Turn the dough out onto a generously floured surface and knead for 2 to 3 minutes to render a smooth ball. Return the dough to the bowl and cover with a thin cloth. Note the time. This is the beginning of the bulk fermentation, which will last approximately 4 hours.

recipe continues »→

Makes 12 sticky buns

For the Leaven

6 tablespoons (56 g) all-purpose flour

6 tablespoons (56 g) whole wheat or spelt flour

Scant ½ cup (112 ml) warm water, about 80°F

Generous 2 tablespoons (40 g) active sourdough starter (see page 105)

For the Dough

¾ cup (175 ml) whole milk

4 tablespoons (½ stick or 57 g) unsalted butter

¼ cup (50 g) granulated sugar

3 cups (390 g) all-purpose flour

⅔ cup (90 g) whole wheat flour

1¾ teaspoons (11 g) salt

2 large eggs, lightly beaten

For the Glaze

¼ cup (½ stick or 57 g) unsalted butter, softened

½ cup (99 g) packed brown sugar

¾ cup (90 g) pecan halves

For the Filling

¼ cup (½ stick or 57 g) unsalted butter, softened

½ cup (99 g) packed brown sugar

1 teaspoon ground cinnamon

← recipe continued from previous page

4. After 45 minutes, do the first set of stretches and folds of the dough. With a wet hand, reach underneath the bottom of the dough, pull the dough up, and fold it over onto itself. Turn the bowl a quarter turn and repeat the stretching and folding. Repeat 2 more times, for a total of 4 turns. (See the picture on page 145 of stretching sourdough bread dough; the sticky bun dough is much stiffer but follows the same general method as the bread.)

5. Repeat this 4-turn stretching and folding about once an hour during the 4-hour bulk fermentation. If the dough becomes too stiff to do the final set of stretches and folds, let it rest for the remainder of the bulk fermentation. At the end of the bulk fermentation, the dough will be more billowy than it was at the beginning.

––––––––––––––– Day 2 ○ 10:30 a.m. –––––––––––––––

1. Make the glaze: In a small bowl, cream the butter and brown sugar. Spread evenly in a large cast-iron skillet or 9 by 13-inch baking pan. Arrange the pecan halves on top.

2. Make the filling: In a small bowl, cream together the butter, brown sugar, and cinnamon.

3. Turn the dough out onto a lightly floured surface. Roll the dough into a 12 by 18-inch rectangle. Spread the filling evenly across the dough. Roll the dough up from a long side into a log. As you roll, push the ends inward a bit to create an even log without tapered ends. Slice into 12 equal pieces with a serrated knife.

4. Place the dough pieces in the pan with the glaze, spacing them out evenly. The gaps between the rolls fill in as the dough rises and expands. Cover with the thin cloth you used earlier. You can either let these rise at room temperature for 3 to 4 hours, until they puff up and touch one another, or you can place them in the refrigerator for a cold proof and bake in the morning (see Note).

––––––––––––– Day 2, afternoon, or Day 3, morning –––––––––––––

Preheat the oven to 375°F. Bake the sticky buns for 20 to 25 minutes, until golden. Invert the pan onto a board. Wait 1 minute, then remove the pan. Serve warm.

Notes

- If baking the next morning, remove the buns from the refrigerator before preheating the oven.

- Start making these buns at any time after your leaven has doubled in size and smells yeasty, fruity, and perhaps slightly sour. This happens between 6 and 12 hours after feeding. Adjust the schedule as desired.

And now for your next recipe . . .

You won't have a crumb of these left to incorporate into another next recipe. But if you haven't done so, feed your starter. Keep it alive with regular feedings so you can continue to make these sticky buns.

Sourdough Zucchini Quick Bread

The unfed sourdough discard is to bakers what zucchini is to gardeners. Whether you nurture a small jar of starter or plant just one zucchini seedling, if you don't find something to cook with your bounty, it will grow unwieldy and you will find yourself overrun with the stuff.

If you keep a sourdough starter *and* you also happen to grow zucchini, this quick bread is for you—or anyone else who loves a homemade, not-too-sweet loaf warm from the oven.

Preheat the oven to 350°F. Generously grease a 9 by 5-inch loaf pan with a little olive oil.

If adding the nuts, toast them for 5 to 10 minutes in the oven, until fragrant but not dark.

In small bowl, combine the flours, salt, cinnamon, baking soda, and baking powder.

In a large bowl, beat the egg until light. Add the sugar, mixing well. Stir in the zucchini, starter, olive oil, and vanilla.

Add the dry ingredients to the zucchini mixture and stir just until combined. Fold in the nuts, if using.

Scrape the batter into the pan and bake for 50 to 60 minutes, until a fork inserted into the center comes out clean. Cool in the pan for 10 minutes, then invert onto a rack to cool completely.

Notes

- You can also use an active starter for this quick bread. Stir it down first to remove the bubbles.

- This recipe also works well with shredded carrots, pumpkin purée (page 271), or overripe bananas. If using bananas, because they are very sweet, reduce the amount of sugar to ½ cup (50 g).

- Ran out of baking powder? If you have baking soda and cream of tartar on hand, combine 2 parts cream of tartar with 1 part baking soda; sift it, then use your homemade baking powder immediately.

Makes 1 loaf

½ cup (65 g) chopped walnuts (optional)

1 cup (130 g) all-purpose flour

½ cup (67 g) whole wheat flour

½ teaspoon salt

1½ teaspoons ground cinnamon

½ teaspoon baking soda

¼ teaspoon baking powder

1 large egg

¾ cup (150 g) sugar

1 cup (140 g) grated zucchini (from 1 zucchini)

½ cup (140 g) sourdough starter discard (see page 105), stirred down (see Note)

⅓ cup (75 ml) olive oil, plus more for greasing the pan

1 teaspoon (5 ml) Bourbon Street Vanilla Extract (page 110) or store-bought

And now for your next recipe . . .

If you have leftover shredded zucchini, use it in the vegetable pancakes on page 172.

Anything Goes Granola

You can easily adapt this recipe to fit what you have on hand. Sweeten it as you like. Stir a spoonful of nut butter into the wet ingredients. Other ingredients to try include flax or hemp seeds, chopped pecans, slivered almonds, pulp rendered from making nut milk (see page 112), dried apples or apricots, a bit of citrus zest (stir in after baking the granola), a few tablespoons of cocoa, or some freshly ground nutmeg. If you bought wheat germ to make the sourdough graham crackers (page 244), toss in a couple tablespoons of that. Regard the proportions listed here as a guide and add various items you find in your pantry (within reason!).

Like many zero-waste swaps, switching from store-bought granola to homemade causes pretty much zero pain—unless you don't make enough and run out immediately. Better make a double batch.

Preheat the oven to 275°F.

In a large bowl, mix the oats, nuts, seeds, coconut, pulp (if using), salt, and cinnamon.

In a small bowl, mix the oil, syrup, and egg white, if using, until well combined.

Pour the wet ingredients into the dry ingredients and combine until all is mixed well. Your hand works best.

Spread the mixture evenly on an ungreased rimmed baking sheet. If you want clumpier granola, press down gently and do not stir during baking. Bake for 30 to 40 minutes, until golden. If you prefer fewer clumps, stir every 15 minutes or so.

Allow to cool on the baking sheet. Break up clumps as desired. Stir in raisins or other dried fruit.

Store in glass jars. The granola will keep for at least 2 weeks.

Makes 6 cups

3 cups old-fashioned rolled oats

1 cup raw whole almonds, pecans, walnuts, pistachios, or hazelnuts, or a mixture of nuts

½ cup raw pumpkin seeds

½ cup raw sunflower seeds

½ cup flaked coconut

½ cup nut milk pulp (optional; see page 112)

½ teaspoon salt

½ teaspoon ground cinnamon

¼ cup coconut oil or unsalted butter, melted, or olive oil

½ cup maple syrup, honey, brown rice syrup, or barley malt syrup

1 large egg white, lightly beaten (optional)

1 cup raisins or other dried fruit

And now for your next recipe . . .

Sprinkle a few spoonfuls of the granola on top of the batter for the sourdough zucchini quick bread (page 157)—or any quick bread or muffin recipe—then bake, for a crunchy topping.

Huevos Rancheros (Salsa-Poached Eggs)

One summer day as I worked on this cookbook, my sister asked me if I had any recipes for tomatoes or eggs. At the time, tomatoes had taken over her garden, thanks in part to her six roaming hens who had pecked around in the soil, eaten bugs and pests, and decimated the compost pile, all the while fertilizing and enriching the soil as they went on their merry way. Every day, the girls also loaded their nesting boxes with fresh eggs filled with rich orange yolks, the product of pastured hens that eat what nature designed hens to eat. I asked Michelle if she'd like a recipe for tomatoes *and* eggs.

Typically eaten at breakfast, this spicy dish of eggs poached in salsa makes a delicious lunch or dinner. Serve it with refried beans (page 180) and sourdough tortillas (page 108) for a satisfying meal.

Heat the olive oil in a large skillet over medium heat. Add the jalapeños and onion and cook until charred, about 5 minutes. Transfer to a food processor or blender.

Add the tomatoes and garlic to the skillet. Cook to soften the tomatoes and lightly brown the garlic, about 5 minutes. Transfer to the food processor or blender. Process the mixture until chunky. (If desired, make the salsa a day or two in advance and store in refrigerator until ready to use.)

Pour the salsa into a large skillet over medium-low heat. Add the tomato paste, salt, cumin, lime juice, and cilantro and stir well, spreading evenly in the pan.

Gently crack the eggs directly onto the top of the tomato mixture, spaced evenly. Cover the skillet and cook until the eggs are just set, 7 to 10 minutes.

Serve immediately with the tortillas.

Serves 3

1 tablespoon olive oil

2 jalapeño peppers, halved

1 small white onion, cut into wedges

1½ pounds ripe tomatoes, chopped (about 3 cups)

2 garlic cloves, peeled

1 tablespoon Worth-It Tomato Paste (page 122) or store-bought

1 teaspoon salt

½ teaspoon ground cumin

1 tablespoon fresh lime juice

¼ cup fresh cilantro, finely chopped

6 large eggs

Tangy and Tender Sourdough Tortillas (page 108), warmed, for serving

And now for your next dish . . .

You may have leftover cilantro on your hands. Make a small amount of the cilantro chutney (see page 184) to eat with savory dishes.

9

Side Dishes
You Can
Commit To

Mon Petit Chou Apple-Ginger Sauerkraut

Cabbages lack sex appeal. These humble vegetables tend not to elicit the same excitement as luscious avocados or tall and slender asparagus spears or smoking-hot hot peppers when we see them at the farmers' market because *we always see them at the farmers' market.* Most of us fall for the vegetables that play hard-to-get, the ones that build anticipation, forcing us to wait six months or eight months or even longer for them to return, beckoning us from the farmstand to enjoy a fleeting taste before they abandon us yet again. We take those dependable, year-round cabbages for granted and put these more alluring vegetables on a pedestal—or, rather, chopping board. If cabbages are the wife, habaneros are the mistress.

But chop those cabbages, salt them, and pack them into jars, and within mere days they will have transcended from unassuming members of the brassica family to tangy, bubbling, and enticing sauerkraut that you can't get enough of. Add chopped apples and grated ginger to the mix, and the honeymoon phase never ends.

Before chopping the cabbage, peel off 1 large outer leaf and set it aside. Quarter the cabbage and slice out the core. Chop the cabbage thinly.

Place the cabbage, apples, and ginger in a large bowl. Sprinkle with the salt.

Grab handfuls of the mixture and squeeze as you combine everything together. Crushing the cabbage and apples helps break down the cell walls, which will release water. Continue to squeeze and crush the cabbage mixture with your hands for a few minutes, until it feels quite wet and the cabbage has become more limp. Taste as you go. If you'd like more salt, sprinkle in a bit more. If it tastes too salty, add more fresh produce. (If you've run out of cabbage and apples, add shredded carrots.)

Makes about 6 cups

1 medium red or green cabbage (about 2½ pounds)

2 medium apples, roughly chopped

1 heaping tablespoon finely grated fresh ginger (about 1 inch)

1 tablespoon salt, plus more to taste

1 teaspoon yellow mustard seeds

recipe continues ⟫→

Place a small plate directly on top of the vegetables. Place a weight over that, such as a jug of water. Allow the vegetables to rest for at least 1 hour while liquid pools in the bottom of the bowl. Drape a towel over everything to keep out impurities.

Remove the weight and plate. You should find a pool of liquid in the bottom of the bowl. Mix in the mustard seeds.

Pack your clean jar. You do not need to sterilize the jars. Choose a jar large enough to hold 6 to 8 cups or pack 2 smaller jars that can each hold 3 to 4 cups (see page 47 for information on choosing jars).

As you fill your jar, pack the wet vegetables tightly with your fist. This will force out air bubbles and submerge the vegetables beneath the liquid. After packing, pour in any liquid remaining in the bowl.

Leave at least 2 inches of space at the top of the jar. Fold the reserved cabbage leaf and stuff it into the jar. (If using two jars, cut the cabbage leaf in two, one half for each jar.) That alone may keep the cabbage mixture submerged in the liquid. If you have a glass weight, place that on the cabbage leaf. A small glass jar, such as a yogurt jar, also works. Closing the lid pushes the small jar down, which pushes the cabbage mixture below the liquid. If you cannot easily close the jar with the smaller jar inside of it, remove some of the vegetables to make more space. If the resting cabbage mixture didn't release enough liquid to completely submerge the cabbage, pour in a bit of water.

Place the jar on a small plate to catch any liquid that may bubble out of the jar during active fermentation. Leave the jar at room temperature for at least 3 days. Carbon dioxide will build up in the jar during the active fermentation of the first several days. During this period, open your jar daily to release the pressure. Sauerkraut will keep in the refrigerator for at least 1 year.

Around day 3, taste the sauerkraut. If you like the taste, move your jar to the refrigerator to slow the fermentation. If you'd prefer a stronger, more sour flavor, leave the jar out for longer, from 2 weeks to 1 month or more. Taste weekly until it has reached the flavor you desire. When you like the taste, the sauerkraut is ready. Move it to the refrigerator. Sauerkraut will keep in the refrigerator for at least 1 year.

Note

If you'd like to make plain sauerkraut, use only cabbage and salt, reduce the salt quantity to 2 teaspoons, and follow the directions as given.

And now for your next recipe . . .

Sauerkraut enlivens the simplest dishes. Add some tangy flavor and crunchy texture to a potato salad or green salad. Tuck it into sandwiches or wraps. Or simply serve it as a healthy condiment with meals.

Lebanese Tabbouleh

Unless you grow your own parsley, you must buy an entire bunch at the grocery store or farmers' market for a recipe that might call for only a few sprigs' worth of the vitamin-rich, dark green leafy herb. In the past, that may have caused you to skip the parsley altogether. But now you have this incredibly fresh, parsley-based salad recipe—tabbouleh. It calls for a large bunch of parsley along with mint, cucumber, tomato, onion, garlic, fresh lemon juice, and olive oil. A bit of bulgur wheat adds a hint of chewiness.

In a small heat-resistant bowl, combine the bulgur and boiling water. Set aside for 1 hour to allow the bulgur to absorb the water.

In a large bowl, combine the parsley, mint, cucumber, tomato, scallions, garlic, olive oil, lemon juice, salt, and pepper to taste.

Drain the bulgur and toss with the salad. Add more salt, lemon juice, or olive oil to taste.

Allow to sit on the counter or place in the refrigerator for 2 to 3 hours to allow the flavors to meld.

And now for your next recipe . . .

Thick parsley stems taste much stronger than their flat leaves. But you can use them here and there rather than composting them all. Brew some tea. Toss a few stems into your stash of vegetable scraps for broth—but only a small handful, as too many of *any* herb will overpower the flavor. Or finely chop some and add to the black-eyed pea and mushroom burgers (page 199), fennel-frond pesto (page 209), or stir-fry (page 181).

Serves 4

½ cup bulgur
(cracked wheat)

½ cup boiling water

1 large bunch fresh
flat-leaf parsley,
leaves finely chopped
(about 2 generous cups)

1 small bunch fresh mint,
leaves finely chopped
(about ¼ cup)

1 medium cucumber,
finely chopped (about 1 cup)

1 medium ripe tomato,
finely chopped (about 1 cup)

½ cup minced scallions,
white and green parts

1 garlic clove, minced

2 tablespoons olive oil,
or more as needed

2 tablespoons fresh
lemon juice (about 1 lemon),
or more as needed

1 teaspoon salt, or more
as needed

Freshly ground black pepper

Sautéed Swiss Chard

It is a truth universally acknowledged that a bunch of chard in possession of good nutrients must be in want of a good recipe.

I would wager a handsome sum that of all the various types of produce, the buy-to-cook ratio of chard runs quite high. We buy leafy greens with the best intentions—we want all those A and K vitamins!—yet delicate greens often languish in the back of the refrigerator until they become compost. This recipe tastes so delicious that you'll want to buy more, not less, chard. Try this recipe also with beet greens or collards.

In a large sauté pan, heat the olive oil over medium heat. Add the garlic and cook, stirring, until golden but not browned, 1 minute.

Add the chard and broth. Turn the heat to high and stir to coat the chard. Cover the skillet and boil for about 5 minutes.

Remove the lid, stir, and continue to cook the chard until all the liquid has cooked off, 2 or 3 minutes.

Add the vinegar, red pepper flakes, and salt and pepper to taste. Serve immediately.

Serves 4

2 tablespoons olive oil

3 garlic cloves, thinly sliced

1 large bunch (about 1 pound) chard, leaves torn into large pieces, stems finely chopped

½ cup unsalted Save-Scraps-Save-Cash Vegetable Broth (page 135)

2 tablespoons red wine vinegar

¼ to ½ teaspoon red pepper flakes

Salt and freshly ground black pepper

And now for your next recipe . . .

This sautéed chard makes a fantastic filling for a savory galette (page 212). Or use the chard to fill dosa-inspired Indian crepes (page 182).

Eat-All-Your-Vegetables Pancakes

While we tell kids constantly to eat all their vegetables, we adults could use that reminder ourselves. These savory vegetable pancakes make both recommendations easy. They satisfy all eaters while clearing a few things out of the refrigerator—half a zucchini, a lone carrot, a pinch of chopped fresh herbs. Have some kale stems left over from a salad? Very finely chop a handful and toss them in. No one will suspect. But almost always include potatoes. You simply cannot go wrong with potatoes, fat, and salt.

If using zucchini or potatoes, place them in the center of a thin dish towel. Roll up the towel and squeeze out the juice. Refrigerate or freeze the liquid for broth.

Place the vegetables in a large bowl and fluff with a fork. Stir in the bread crumbs, eggs, salt, and pepper to taste and combine well.

Heat a large skillet over medium heat and add enough oil to coat it.

For each pancake, drop ¼ cup of the batter into the hot pan. With a spatula, flatten it down so it's about ¼ inch thick. Flip after the bottom has browned, about 5 minutes. Remove from the pan once the other side has also browned, another 3 to 5 minutes.

Add more oil to the pan as necessary and continue cooking the pancakes. Keep them warm in the oven all together, or serve individually at once.

Serve with sour cream (see page 118), egg white aioli (page 127), or cilantro chutney (see page 184), if desired.

Makes twelve 3-inch pancakes

4 cups grated vegetables, such as russet potatoes, carrots, zucchini, sweet potatoes, turnips, parsnips, or cabbage

¼ cup bread crumbs or flour (all-purpose, whole wheat, or rye)

2 large eggs

1 teaspoon coarse salt

Freshly ground black pepper

Olive oil, for frying

And now for your next recipe . . .

If you've made the kimchi (page 187), drain and chop some finely for a spicy kimchi version of these pancakes. Omit the salt here, as kimchi tastes quite salty. If necessary, add salt to taste.

Garlicky Dilly Beans

The first time you ferment dilly beans, you feel like a wizard. Essentially, you place a bunch of garlic and fresh dill into a clean jar, stuff fresh green beans on top, and pour in salted water. You close the jar, set it aside on the kitchen counter, and wait. The contents of the jar will soon bubble to life and change from clear to cloudy—both signs of a successful fermentation under way. After a week or so, you taste your beans. They will have transformed into a tangy, crunchy appetizer, teeming with beneficial cultures. You may begin to wonder what other magical powers you possess.

Combine the water and salt in a large measuring cup. Set aside. The salt will dissolve as you prepare the beans.

Snap off the stem ends of the beans or line them up on your cutting board and cut them off. Don't bother trimming the tails.

Place the garlic, dill, peppercorns, and red pepper flakes in either one 6- to 8-cup jar or two 1-quart jars (see page 47 on selecting jars).

Line the beans up neatly and stuff them into the jar. Pour the salted water over top. If the beans float up, place a weight on top of them. A tiny glass bowl or small glass yogurt jar works well. Close the lid.

Place the jar on a small plate to catch any liquid that may bubble out of the jar during active fermentation. Set the jar aside at room temperature. As the beans ferment, the liquid in the jar will become cloudy and the beans will darken in color. Taste the beans after 1 week. Let them ferment longer if you'd like them less crunchy.

Store the dilly beans in the refrigerator, where they will keep for several months, if not longer.

Makes 2 quarts

4 cups water

3 tablespoons salt

1 pound fresh green, yellow, or purple beans

4 garlic cloves, smashed

6 sprigs fresh dill

½ teaspoon whole peppercorns

¼ teaspoon red pepper flakes

And now for your next recipe . . .

After you've eaten your dilly beans, save the cultured brine to:

○ **Ferment more vegetables.** Place whole vegetables in the jar of brine, weight them down , close the lid, and wait. Or add a bit of brine to a batch of ketchup (see page 126) to kick-start the fermentation.

○ **Drink.** People at my farmers' market pay a lot of money for bottled brine. A daily shot of it provides a large dose of living cultures. You get your probiotic brine as a by-product of your dilly beans.

○ **Stir some flavor into soup.** The beneficial microbes die when heated, but the soup tastes good.

○ **Liven up** hummus and dips, potato salads, dressings, and so on.

Hearty and Herby
Roasted Vegetables

If you have roasted vegetables on hand, then you can throw together a scrumptious meal quickly. I roast vegetables a couple of times a week, usually with the intent of transforming many of them into another dish later. For example, on the first night we might eat some of the roasted vegetables as a side dish. Then later in the week, the roasted vegetables might become filling for the frittata (page 207). I might then purée the last handful of them to add to a batch of hummus (page 248).

The number of vegetables you roast at any one time is limited to the number of baking sheets or pans you have and the number of racks in your oven. But don't let that stop you.

Preheat the oven to 400°F.

Because vegetables roast for different periods of time, place each type on its own baking sheet, in a large cast-iron pan, or in a glass baking dish.

Drizzle on the olive oil and toss with your hands to coat well. Spread each vegetable in a single layer on the baking sheet, leaving a little space between. (Piled up on top of one another, the pieces will become soft, not roasted.) Top with the sprigs of fresh herbs or sprinkle with the dry herbs, followed by the salt to taste. Top with the garlic.

Place the baking sheet in the oven and stir or shake the pan every 15 minutes or so. Roast the softer vegetables, such as mushrooms, zucchini, and tomatoes, for 15 to 20 minutes and the root vegetables, such as beets, potatoes, and carrots, for 30 to 60 minutes. The vegetables are ready when the pieces are tender and browned around the edges.

Yield varies

Vegetables of choice, such as potatoes, sweet potatoes, butternut squash, acorn squash, pumpkin, beets, carrots, parsnips, Brussels sprouts, mushrooms, eggplant, zucchini, bell peppers, tomatoes, and onions, cut into bite-size pieces

½ tablespoon olive oil per 1 cup chopped vegetables

Sprigs of fresh rosemary or thyme, cumin seed, or herbes de Provence

Salt

1 garlic clove, smashed, for each batch of vegetables

And now for your next recipe . . .

Use any extra roasted vegetables to get a head start on the shepherd's pie (page 193) or the savory galette (page 212). To make soup with your roasted vegetables, purée them with water or broth in a blender or with an immersion blender in a deep pot (to avoid splattering the walls). Start with a small amount of liquid and add more until your soup has reached the desired consistency.

Tangy Tomato Salsa

This tangy, intensely fresh, and slightly effervescent salsa ferments quickly, usually within a couple of days. Although you may prefer to blanch and peel the tomatoes for a smooth and silky cooked sauce, please skip those steps for this recipe! You won't detect the peels in the finished salsa and the boiling water would kill some of the beneficial bacteria on the peels that are required to ferment this.

Vary the ingredients listed here according to taste. Have a couple of extra bell peppers on hand? Toss them in. Forgot to buy the bell peppers? That's fine, too. Peaches taste delicious in this, so replace one-third to one-half of the tomatoes with an equivalent amount of peaches. Add more hot peppers if you prefer your salsa very hot.

Place the tomatoes in a large bowl. Use your hands to crush them into a soupy consistency. This takes only a few minutes. Stir in the bell pepper, onion, garlic, jalapeño, cilantro, lime juice, and salt. Taste. If you'd like more salt, stir in a bit more.

Pack the salsa into clean jars (see page 47 on selecting jars), leaving approximately 2 inches of headspace. Close the lids. Place the jars on plates to catch any liquid that bubbles out during active fermentation. Set aside at room temperature.

Open the jars daily (i.e., burp them) to release the carbon dioxide building up inside.

Taste after 2 days. If the solids have separated and floated to the top of the jar, it's likely ready, with a tangy flavor. If you like the taste, place your jars in the refrigerator to slow down the fermentation. If it's not ready, stir it down and let it ferment a little longer and check the flavor again in 12 to 24 hours.

Do not let the salsa ferment for more than several days, as the tomatoes or any fruit you've added can turn alcoholic quickly.

Makes about 8 cups

3 pounds ripe tomatoes, cored and chopped into bite-size pieces (about 6 cups)

1 to 2 bell peppers, cored, seeded, and chopped

1 white onion, chopped

6 garlic cloves, minced

1 to 2 jalapeño or serrano peppers, minced

½ cup fresh cilantro, chopped

4 tablespoons fresh lime or lemon juice (from 2 limes or lemons)

1 tablespoon salt, plus more to taste

Note

To speed up your work, use a food processor to chop the tomatoes; however, do not process the onion, as that can make it taste bitter.

And now for your next recipe . . .

If you have leftover salsa, use it to poach an egg or two, as you do for the huevos rancheros (page 161), or add a bit of the salsa to a pot of chili (page 222).

Restaurant-Style
Refried Beans

The first time my daughter Mary Kat made refried beans for us and described her recipe, I asked, "Is that all you do?!" I had only ever eaten refried beans from either a restaurant or a can. I had never made them myself. I've made them often since then.

These refried beans are a must to serve on the side with huevos rancheros (page 161). If you have unfed sourdough discard, consider making the sourdough tortillas (page 108) as well. Plan your meal several days in advance, and you can also serve it with the tepache (page 258) for a Mexican-themed meal.

Soak the beans in water to cover for at least 6 hours. Drain and rinse the beans. Cook according to directions on page 132 (bean cooking times vary from a few minutes in a pressure cooker to 8 hours in a slow cooker). Drain the cooked beans, separately reserving the beans and liquid. (Do this a day or more in advance, if desired.)

Place the cooked beans in a large saucepan over medium heat. Add the oil, garlic, tomatoes, pepper, cumin, chili powder, salt, and pepper to taste. Stir and mash the beans and tomatoes with a potato masher. Add some of the reserved bean liquid for a thinner consistency, if desired.

Continue to cook, stirring and mashing, until the beans begin to bubble and the mixture thickens. Serve. Leftovers can be stored in the refrigerator for at least 5 days.

Serves 4

2 cups dried pinto beans or black beans, or 5 cups cooked beans

¼ cup olive oil, coconut oil, or unsalted butter

2 garlic cloves, minced

1 cup chopped ripe tomato

1 jalapeño or serrano pepper, minced

2 teaspoons ground cumin

½ teaspoon homemade chili powder (page 98) or store-bought

1 teaspoon salt, or more as needed

Freshly ground black pepper

And now for your next recipe . . .

If you and your family have not polished off all these refried beans, consider making a simple dip of the remainder. Purée the bean mixture with a small amount of sour cream (see page 118), hot sauce (page 91), and/or the fermented tomato salsa (page 179), and adjust to taste.

Customizable Stir-Fry
with Peanut Sauce

This recipe will get more vegetables out of your refrigerator and into the tummies of your family. Disguised as a smooth, gingery, nutty peanut sauce, the "bait" in this recipe will lure even the fiercest vegetable detractors to the table. Make the peanut sauce a day or two in advance, if desired.

Make the peanut sauce: In a medium bowl, thoroughly combine the peanut butter, ginger, garlic, lime juice, soy sauce, kombucha, honey, sesame oil, and red pepper flakes. Thin with hot water, 1 tablespoon at a time, to reach your desired consistency (about 2 tablespoons should do it, but add more if you want).

Make the stir-fry: Heat a wok or skillet over medium heat. Add the peanuts and cook, stirring, until fragrant, about 5 minutes.

Heat 1 tablespoon of the peanut oil in the wok over medium heat. Add the spinach, if using, and stir-fry until wilted, 1 to 2 minutes. Transfer to a plate.

Add the remaining 1 tablespoon oil to the wok. Add the onion, garlic, and ginger. Salt lightly and sauté for about 5 minutes, until softened. Increase the heat to medium high, add the chopped vegetables, and stir constantly until tender-crisp, 3 to 5 minutes.

Add the peanut sauce to the pan along with the spinach (if using). Toss gently to evenly coat the vegetables with the sauce, and heat through. Stir in the toasted peanuts and serve with the rice.

And now for your next recipe . . .

Leftover rice makes excellent fried rice. If you have leftover rice after you've made this stir-fry, store it for a day or two in the refrigerator to dry out a bit, and then make the kimchi fried rice (page 203) for lunch or dinner.

Serves 3

For the Peanut Sauce
½ cup creamy peanut butter (page 130)

1 (1-inch) piece fresh ginger, finely minced or grated

1 large garlic clove, finely minced or grated

2 tablespoons fresh lime juice (from 1 lime)

2 teaspoons soy sauce

2 tablespoons vinegary but still somewhat sweet kombucha (page 255) or rice wine vinegar

1 teaspoon honey, molasses, or sugar

1 tablespoon toasted sesame oil

¼ teaspoon red pepper flakes

For the Stir-Fry
½ cup unsalted, unroasted peanuts

2 tablespoons peanut oil

1 cup fresh spinach or sliced bok choy (optional)

1 medium onion, thinly sliced

4 garlic cloves, minced

1 teaspoon minced fresh ginger

Salt

4 cups chopped vegetables of choice, such as broccoli, carrots, celery, bell peppers, mushrooms, or green beans

3 cups cooked rice, warmed

Make-Ahead Dosa Batter
and Indian Crepes

I love these savory, sourdough-like Indian crepes for so many reasons. First, fermentation increases the digestibility of both the rice and the dal in these crepes. Second, this recipe enables you to sneak more protein-rich lentils into your family's diet—a legume that's good for both our health and the planet's. Third, although you do need to plan ahead to make these, once the batter ferments, you can store it in the refrigerator for up to a week. Then it's dosas on demand!

Although traditional dosa recipes call for urad dal, this slightly heretical recipe uses whatever lentils you have on hand, because (a) you will have trouble finding urad dal in bulk and (b) we're trying to be flexible for the times you just need to offload a random ½ cup of lentils. You can make these with various types of rice as well—long-grain, short-grain, white, brown, wild. If you have any little bits of chopped hot peppers, onions, or cilantro on hand, add them to the batter just before cooking for a variation.

When the batter is ready, arm yourself with a metal measuring cup to swirl it out on the hot pan. Your swirling technique will improve with practice, which gives you a good excuse to make these delectable Indian-style crepes often.

Make the batter: In a medium bowl, soak the rice, lentils, fenugreek seeds (if using), and water to cover overnight at room temperature, or for at least 6 hours. Drain and rinse.

Combine the rice-lentil mixture with 1½ cups of the water in a food processor or blender and grind until smooth. This can take up to 10 minutes. Add another ¼ to ½ cup water, until you have the consistency of cream.

Makes about twenty 7-inch dosas

For the Batter

2 cups brown rice

1 cup urad dal or other dried lentil, such as moong dal or masoor dal

1 teaspoon fenugreek seeds (optional)

About 2 cups water

1½ teaspoons salt

For the Dosas

Ghee (clarified butter) or coconut oil (or other oil with a high smoking point), melted

Pour the batter into a non-reactive bowl and cover with a plate. Allow to sit in a warm spot to ferment for up to 24 hours or longer, depending on your kitchen environment. Check the batter every 8 hours or so. If you've used a glass bowl, you can check it with a glance. The batter is ready when it has risen, is filled with bubbles, and tastes sour.

Stir in the salt and either cook immediately or store the batter in the refrigerator for up to 1 week.

Make the dosas: Over medium heat, lightly coat a very well-seasoned cast-iron skillet with the ghee.

Pour ¼ cup of the batter into the center of the pan with a metal measuring cup. Wait 5 seconds for the batter to stick to the pan. Then, use the bottom of the measuring cup to gently swirl the batter in a circular motion. Begin in the center and spread outward until you've made a very thin, 7- to 8-inch-wide circle. Drizzle between ¼ and ½ teaspoon of ghee over the dosa.

Cook until the edges begin to dry and pull away from the pan and the bottom of the dosa turns golden, about 2 minutes. Flip it over. Cook for 1 to 2 minutes more. Transfer to a plate.

Continue to cook the dosas and either keep them warm in the oven all together or serve them individually immediately. (Store any remaining batter in the refrigerator. If it thickens during storage, thin it out with a bit of water before cooking.)

And now for your next recipe . . .

Serve these dosas on the side with chana masala (page 197) or the cauliflower and potato dal (page 217); fill your dosas with the potato filling of the empamosas (see page 184); or dip these dosas in the cilantro chutney (see page 184).

Empamosas
with Cilantro Chutney

After making these empanada-inspired, samosa-filled hand pies, one of my kids asked me what made them zero waste. I could have said that the taste of the savory, spicy, samosa-type filling tucked inside flaky pastry guarantees that no empamosa will go uneaten. But really, I just love the *method*. You can fill hand pies with all kinds of ingredients, based on what you have, to help you use up everything and waste nothing.

Did you make the chili (page 222) or the chana masala (page 197) and want to create something new out of them? Cook them down to a thick consistency and your filling is ready. Or fill hand pies with refried beans (page 180) mixed with a bit of strained fermented tomato salsa (page 179). For dessert, stuff hand pies with chopped apples that have been cooked down in butter, sugar, cinnamon, and nutmeg.

If desired, make the chutney for these savory empamosas a day or two in advance.

Preheat the oven to 375°F.

Make the empamosas: Place the potatoes and carrot in a medium pot and add enough water to cover by 1 inch. Add 1 teaspoon of salt. Cover and bring to a boil, then lower the heat for a vigorous simmer. Continue to simmer, uncovered, until the vegetables are fork-tender, 10 to 15 minutes. Drain and set aside.

Return the pot to the stove. Add the oil and heat over medium heat. Add the cumin seeds and cook, stirring until fragrant, about 1 minute. Add the onion, garlic, ginger, and pepper. Cook, stirring occasionally, until the onion is softened, about 5 minutes.

Add the turmeric, coriander, garam masala, and mustard seeds and stir to coat with the onion mixture. Cook, stirring occasionally, until fragrant, about 1 minute. Add the potatoes and carrot and stir

Makes 12 empamosas

For the Empamosas

¾ pound red potatoes, unpeeled, cut into 1-inch pieces

1 medium carrot, chopped

1½ teaspoons salt, plus more as needed

1 tablespoon coconut oil

½ teaspoon cumin seeds

1 medium onion, chopped (about 1 cup)

1 garlic clove, minced

1 teaspoon minced fresh ginger

1 serrano or jalapeño pepper, minced

½ teaspoon ground turmeric

½ teaspoon ground coriander

¼ teaspoon garam masala

½ teaspoon yellow mustard seeds

1½ teaspoons lime or lemon juice (from 1 lime or lemon)

¼ cup finely chopped fresh cilantro

Double recipe No-Fear Pastry (page 107), chilled

recipe and ingredients continue ⟶

←« recipe continued from previous page

to coat, mashing the potatoes a bit with a wooden spoon. Add the lime juice, cilantro, and the remaining ½ teaspoon salt and adjust to taste.

On a lightly floured surface, cut the pastry into 12 equal pieces. Roll each piece into a ball and flatten into a disk. With a rolling pin, roll each disk into a 5-inch circle.

Place a generous 2 tablespoons of filling in the middle of each circle. Fold the dough in half to form a half-moon. Beginning with one end of the empamosa, fold the edge onto itself, one thumb-size amount of dough at a time (see picture below). Continue doing this all along the edge of the half-moon.

Place the empamosas on an ungreased cookie sheet. Continue to fill and shape the remaining dough circles.

Bake in the oven for about 20 minutes, until the pastry is golden.

Make the chutney: Place the cilantro, garlic, hot peppers, lime juice, salt, and sugar in a food processor and process until a smooth purée; this can take several minutes. Serve with the empamosas.

For the Cilantro Chutney

2 cups packed fresh cilantro leaves and stems

2 large garlic cloves, smashed

2 serrano or jalapeño peppers

2 tablespoons fresh lime or lemon juice (from I lime or lemon)

½ teaspoon salt

½ teaspoon sugar

And now for your next recipe . . .

You may have a bit of extra filling on hand. In a cast-iron pan or skillet, heat a small amount of oil over medium heat. Add the leftover filling and cook, but don't stir, until the potatoes turn golden brown. Flip and cook the other side. Serve your pan-fried potatoes with any leftover chutney. The chutney also goes well with the vegetable pancakes (page 172) or the Indian crepes (dosas) on page 182.

SIDE DISHES YOU CAN COMMIT TO ∘ THE ZERO-WASTE CHEF

Simple Spicy Kimchi

The real trick to making amazing-tasting kimchi—spicy fermented cabbage beloved originally in Korea and now everywhere—is procuring gochugaru, a bright red, fairly coarse, hot, sweet, and smoky spice. You can, of course, substitute a smaller amount of cayenne pepper or red pepper flakes, but your kimchi won't have the same distinctive flavor. Look for the gochugaru in Asian markets and upscale grocery stores. The type of cabbage you use also affects the flavor of your kimchi. Red or green cabbage or Savoy *will* ferment— you can't stop cabbages from fermenting!—but they will lack the slightly sweet taste of napa cabbage, also known as Chinese cabbage.

Peel off 1 cabbage leaf and set it aside. Beginning at the top of the cabbage, cut it into 2-inch-wide pieces.

In a large bowl, toss together the cabbage, radish, and scallions. Sprinkle on the salt.

Squeeze handfuls of the vegetables as you mix everything. This crushing helps breaks down the cell walls, which will release water. Continue to squeeze the vegetables for a few minutes until they feel quite wet and the cabbage has become somewhat limp. Taste. If you'd like more salt, sprinkle in a bit more. If it tastes too salty, you can remedy this by adding more cabbage.

Place a plate over the vegetables and place a weight on the plate, such as a jug filled with water. Cover the bowl with a towel and let the vegetables sit for a couple of hours.

While the vegetables rest, in a separate bowl, combine the garlic, ginger, gochugaru, and kelp granules (if using).

Remove the weight and plate from the cabbage. You should find liquid pooling in the bottom of the bowl. Add the spice mixture to the vegetables and combine everything well.

Makes 4 cups

1 (2-pound) napa cabbage

1 (1-pound) daikon radish, cut into 2-inch-long matchsticks that are ⅛ inch thick

4 scallions (white and green parts), cut into 1-inch pieces

1 tablespoon plus 2 teaspoons salt, or more as needed

6 garlic cloves, minced

1 (1-inch) piece fresh ginger, minced or grated

¼ cup gochugaru

1 teaspoon dried kelp granules (optional)

recipe continues ⟶

Pack the kimchi into a jar large enough to hold 6 cups or pack two smaller jars that can each hold 3 to 4 cups (see page 47 on choosing jars). Pack the vegetables into the jar tightly. This will force out air bubbles and submerge the vegetables in the liquid. I use my bare hands for this, but depending on the spices and how much you put in, you may want to use a large wooden spoon, pestle, or, if you have one, a wooden pounder. After packing, pour in any liquid remaining in the bowl.

Leave at least 2 inches of space at the top of the jar. Stuff the reserved cabbage leaf into the jar. (If using two jars, cut the cabbage leaf in two and use half for each jar.) That alone may keep the kimchi submerged in the liquid. If you have a glass weight, place that on the cabbage leaf. A small glass jar such as a yogurt jar also works. Closing the lid pushes the small jar down, which shoves the cabbage mixture below the surface of the liquid. If you cannot easily close the jar with the small jar inside of it, remove some of the vegetables to make more space.

Napa cabbage contains a lot of water. In the unlikely event that the resting cabbage did not release enough liquid and the kimchi is not completely submerged in the jar, pour a bit of water in until you've covered the vegetables.

Place the jar on a small plate to catch any liquid that may bubble out during active fermentation. Leave the jar at room temperature for at least 3 days.

Carbon dioxide will build up in the jar during the active fermentation, which will likely begin on day 1. During this period, open your jar daily to release the pressure. Taste daily. Depending on your kitchen, your kimchi will be ready in about 3 days. Move it to the refrigerator. It will keep for several months but tastes best if eaten within 2 months.

And now for your next recipe . . .

Don't toss that overly ripe, aged kimchi! Make kimchi soup: Heat 2 tablespoons oil in a large pot. Sauté 1 chopped onion and 2 minced garlic cloves for 5 minutes. Add 4 cups of vegetable broth (see page 135), 1 cup of kimchi, and 1 cup chopped fresh kale. Heat through and add soy sauce to taste. To serve, ladle the soup into bowls, top with a poached egg, and garnish with chopped scallions.

THE ZERO-WASTE CHEF ◦ 189 ◦ SIDE DISHES YOU CAN COMMIT TO

10

Make Mains,
Not Waste

Feed-the-Flock Bean and Mushroom Shepherd's Pie

While we can all agree that mashed potatoes taste delicious on a shepherd's pie, we may disagree on how to mash those potatoes. Essentially, we have a three-party potato-mashing system in this country. The food millers and potato ricers split the smooth-and-creamy vote, which poses a problem if the cook elected to prepare the mashed potatoes at Thanksgiving falls on the other side of the mashing spectrum and wields a straightforward potato masher. And of course, some independents simply mash with a fork. No candidate who attempts to use a food processor has ever made it onto the ballot, owing to the gluey mess that the machine's blades render.

If you use a food mill, you can cook the potatoes unpeeled—the food mill removes the skins. If you *prefer* peels in your mashed potatoes, mash the potatoes with a masher or fork.

If using dried beans, soak them for at least 6 hours. Cook according to directions on page 132 (bean cooking times vary from a few minutes in a pressure cooker to 8 hours in a slow cooker). Drain the cooked beans, and separately reserve the beans and broth.

Peel the potatoes, if desired (or if using a potato ricer). Place the potatoes in a medium saucepan and add enough cold water to cover by 1 inch or so. Add 2 teaspoons of the salt. Cover and bring to a boil, then reduce the heat to maintain a vigorous simmer, and simmer, uncovered, until the potatoes are fork-tender, 15 to 20 minutes. You want them soft enough to mash. Drain the potatoes in a colander, reserving the liquid for another dish, if desired.

Place the butter, milk, and 1 teaspoon of the salt in the empty saucepan. Heat until the butter just melts, then turn off the heat.

Serves 4 to 6

- 1¼ cups dried black beans or black-eyed peas, or 3 cups cooked beans or peas
- 2 pounds Yukon Gold potatoes
- 3½ teaspoons salt, plus more to taste
- Freshly ground black pepper
- 6 tablespoons (¾ stick) unsalted butter, cut into ¼-inch slices
- ¾ cup whole milk, half-and-half, or nut or seed milk (see page 112)
- Freshly ground black pepper
- 3 tablespoons olive oil
- 3 medium carrots, diced
- 2½ cups chopped winter vegetables of choice, such as turnips, parsnips, or squash
- 10 ounces cremini (brown) mushrooms, sliced (about 4 cups)
- 1 large yellow or white onion, or 3 medium shallots, diced
- 1 garlic clove, minced
- ¼ cup Worth-It Tomato Paste (page 122) or store-bought
- 1 cup dry red wine (see Note)
- 1 sprig fresh rosemary, leaves stripped and chopped
- 1 sprig fresh thyme, leaves stripped and chopped
- 1 bay leaf

recipe continues »→

←« recipe continued from previous page

Process the potatoes in the food mill or potato ricer directly over the saucepan, or place the potatoes in the pot and mash with a potato masher or fork. Stir to combine well, then season with pepper and more salt to taste, if necessary.

Heat 1 tablespoon of the olive oil over medium heat in a large sauté pan. Sauté the carrots and winter vegetables until slightly softened, 5 to 10 minutes. Transfer to a bowl.

Add the remaining 2 tablespoons oil to the sauté pan. Sauté the mushrooms until they begin to release liquid, 5 to 8 minutes. Add the onion and garlic, then sauté until softened, 5 to 10 minutes more. Stir in the tomato paste. Add the wine, bring to a simmer, and stir, scraping up browned bits in the bottom of the pan. Simmer for a few minutes.

Add the cooked beans along with 1 cup of their cooking liquid. Stir in the rosemary, thyme, bay leaf, the remaining ½ teaspoon salt, and pepper to taste. Simmer for about 20 minutes, until the liquid reduces by about half.

Preheat the oven to 350°F. Lightly grease a 9 by 13-inch baking dish.

Remove the bay leaf from the bean mixture. Spread the mixture evenly in the baking dish.

Layer the vegetable mixture evenly over the beans. Layer the mashed potatoes evenly over the vegetables.

Place the baking dish on a baking sheet to catch any bubbling juices and bake for 30 to 40 minutes, until the potatoes begin to brown.

Note

If desired, use more of the bean cooking water in place of the wine.

And now for your next recipe . . .

Wine rarely goes to waste, but if you have some left over from making this shepherd's pie, use it to replace some of the liquid in the chili (page 222); the wine adds a rich flavor to the dish.

Takeout-Style Chana Masala

This iconic Indian dish, made with chickpeas simmered in a spicy, tomato-onion sauce, brings everyone together—poor students and rich techies, picky kids and hungry adults, vegans and omnivores. In addition to bridging our differences, this simple dish serves as a great example of kitchen efficiency. I cook the chickpeas a day or more in advance in my pressure cooker, with an extra cup of chickpeas tossed in to whip up hummus (page 248) or roasted chickpeas (page 240) later in the week. In winter, I use a jar of roasted tomatoes that I squirreled away in the freezer at the end of summer. I also often double the recipe for a cook-once-eat-twice yield. Like soups and stews, the flavor of this simple dish only improves on the second day. Chana masala also freezes well.

If using dried chickpeas, soak them for at least 6 hours. Drain and cook according to instructions on page 132 (bean cooking times vary from a few minutes in a pressure cooker to 8 hours in a slow cooker). Drain the cooked chickpeas.

If using fresh tomatoes, bring a large pot of water to a boil, dip the tomatoes in one by one, for 1 minute, then remove and place on a plate to briefly cool. Slip off the skins and cut the tomatoes into 1-inch pieces. (Or, if using the roasted tomatoes, run them through a food mill.)

In a large skillet, Dutch oven, or deep sauté pan, heat the oil over medium heat. Add the cumin seeds and cook, stirring, until fragrant, about 1 minute. Add the onion, garlic, ginger, and peppers. Cook, stirring occasionally, until the onion has softened, 5 to 10 minutes.

Add the garam masala, coriander, turmeric, and salt and stir for 1 minute. Stir in the tomatoes, breaking them up with the back of a wooden spoon. If using fresh tomatoes, cook for about 5 minutes; if using roasted tomatoes, no extra cooking is needed.

Serves 4

1¼ cups dried chickpeas, or 3¾ cups cooked chickpeas

2 pounds ripe tomatoes, peeled and chopped (about 4 cups; see Note), or 2 cups roasted tomatoes (page 121)

2 tablespoons coconut oil or olive oil

1 teaspoon cumin seeds

1 medium onion, diced

4 garlic cloves, minced

4 teaspoons minced fresh ginger

1 to 2 serrano or jalapeño peppers, minced

2 teaspoons garam masala

1 teaspoon ground coriander

½ teaspoon ground turmeric

1 teaspoon salt, or more as needed

½ cup water

2 to 4 tablespoons fresh lemon or lime juice (from 1 to 2 lemons or limes)

½ cup fresh cilantro, roughly chopped, plus more for garnish

4 cups cooked rice or 12 Indian crepes (dosas; page 182), for serving

Pick-Your-Peppers Hot Sauce (optional; page 91)

Preserved lemons (optional; page 95)

recipe continues »→

←◄ recipe continued from previous page

Stir in the cooked chickpeas and the water. Bring to a simmer, then reduce the heat to medium low and simmer, uncovered, stirring occasionally, until the sauce has thickened slightly, about 20 minutes.

Turn off the heat and stir in the lemon juice and cilantro. Garnish with a bit of extra cilantro and serve with the rice or crepes; if desired, accompany with hot pepper sauce and preserved lemons.

Note

Although it will render a smoother sauce, peeling the fresh tomatoes is optional in this and other tomato-based recipes.

And now for your next recipe . . .

You may not want to be bothered to peel the tomatoes for this dish. But if you do, hold on to those skins and dehydrate them for the savory popcorn seasoning (page 247).

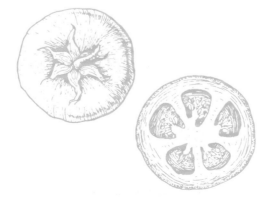

Black-Eyed Pea and Mushroom Burgers

Creamy black-eyed peas make a delicious base for these bean burgers, and the cooked-down mushrooms add loads of flavor. Ground-up oats act as a binder to keep the burger patties together.

If you want burger buns for these, you can buy them—you don't have to make everything yourself. It's okay! You have no moral obligation to grow the wheat to grind the grain to make the flour to make the buns. Your local bakery may sell fresh buns loose that you can put in your own bag. But if you want to bake the buns, you'll find a recipe on page 96. You can also wrap the burgers in lettuce. Or crumble them up and eat them in a soft tortilla (page 108).

Makes 12 small patties

1¼ cups dried black-eyed peas, or 3 cups cooked peas

8 ounces cremini (brown) mushrooms, roughly chopped (about 3 cups)

4 tablespoons olive oil

1 small onion, chopped

2 garlic cloves, minced

1½ teaspoons ground cumin

½ teaspoon homemade chili powder (page 98) or store-bought

1 teaspoon salt

1 cup rolled oats, plus more as needed

Stepped-Up Ketchup (page 126), As You Like It Honey Mustard (page 129), egg white aioli (page 127), Simple Spicy Kimchi (page 187), or toppings of choice

If using dried black-eyed peas, soak them for at least 6 hours. Drain and cook according to directions on page 132 (bean cooking times vary from a few minutes in a pressure cooker to 8 hours in a slow cooker). Drain the cooked black-eyed peas.

Preheat the oven to 350°F. Grease two baking sheets.

In a medium skillet over medium heat, sauté the mushrooms in 3 tablespoons of the olive oil until cooked down and the water is released, 5 to 8 minutes. Transfer to a large bowl.

Add the remaining 1 tablespoon oil to the skillet. Cook the onion and garlic, stirring occasionally, until softened, 5 to 10 minutes. Add the cumin, chili powder, and salt and cook, stirring, for 1 minute.

Place the oats in a food processor and process for about 30 seconds, to render a coarse oat flour. Add the onion-garlic mixture and 2 cups of the cooked black-eyed peas. Pulse several times until less coarse but not smooth.

recipe continues ⤜→

←« recipe continued from previous page

Add the blended mixture to the bowl with the mushrooms. Add the remaining 1 cup of black-eyed peas. If the mixture is too sticky to form patties, process and add another 1 to 2 tablespoons of oats.

Wet your hands, then roll ¼ cup of the mixture into a ball. Flatten the ball in the middle with your fingers as you rotate it and use your thumb to flatten the edges. Place on the baking sheet and continue to roll and shape the remaining burgers.

Bake for 12 minutes. Flip the burgers over and bake for another 12 minutes, or until crispy. (Alternatively, you can cook these in a skillet on the stovetop in a bit of oil.) Serve with ketchup, mustard, aioli, kimchi, or toppings of choice.

And now for your next dish . . .

If you've soaked and cooked the black-eyed peas, save the cooking broth! If you won't use it right away, freeze it in either wide-mouth jars or in ice cube trays and grab the cubes as you need them. Use the broth to add flavor and to thicken soups, such as the ribollita (page 225) or use some to cook your lentils for the cauliflower and potato dal (page 217).

Kimchi Fried Rice

I know I have a hit recipe on my hands when my kids can't respond to my "How does it taste?" question because, on the one hand, they don't want to stop eating, and on the other, I've taught them not to talk with their mouths full of food. They simply nod or give me a thumbs up with their free hand, while busily wielding their forks with the other.

This is one of those recipes.

And it is *so* easy to make. If you've made the kimchi on page 187, you've already done most of the work. Thank your earlier self for having such foresight. Have some leftover rice in the refrigerator? Dinner is coming right up.

In a large, deep skillet, heat the oil over medium-high heat. Add the onions and sauté until translucent, about 3 minutes. Add the kimchi and sauté for 2 more minutes. Add the rice, kimchi juice, soy sauce, and sesame oil. Stir to break up any clumps of rice and to coat it with liquid.

Make a well in the center of the mixture. Pour in the eggs, then scramble for 2 to 3 minutes and stir into the kimchi and rice until the eggs are cooked through. Season to taste with salt.

Notes

- Leftover rice works best with this dish. You want it to have begun to dry out so it won't lump together the way freshly cooked, fluffy rice would.

- You may not have ¼ cup of kimchi juice in your jar. Just remove as much as you can.

Serves 3

¼ cup coconut or peanut oil

2 small onions, chopped

2 cups Simple Spicy Kimchi (page 187), roughly chopped, with ¼ cup kimchi juice (see Note)

4 cups leftover cooked white rice (see Note)

2 tablespoons soy sauce

2 tablespoons sesame oil

4 large eggs, lightly beaten

4 scallions (green and white parts), sliced, for garnish

Salt

SYS
(Save Your Scraps)

While chopping the scallions, save an inch or so of the root ends and place them in a jar of water to regrow. Once they have grown a few inches, place them in a pot of soil sitting outside or in a sunny window. Simply water them when the soil dries out, and occasionally feed them a layer of compost. Snip off the green shoots as needed.

Farro and Kale Salad
with Preserved Lemon
and Dried Apricots

When I rave about my preserved lemons (see page 95)—which I do often—people inevitably ask, "But what do you *do* with preserved lemons?" For one thing, you make a giant bowl of this farro and kale salad. And make it often.

Combine the warm farro with the dressing to absorb the flavors of the preserved lemon, fresh lemon juice, and olive oil. Toss in chopped dried apricots, kale ribbons and, if you have any stale bread on hand, whir that up in a food processor, toast the resulting bread crumbs quickly in a dry pan on the stove, and sprinkle on the salad just before serving for a satisfying crunch.

Salt the water and bring it to a boil in a pot. Add the farro, turn the heat down to a simmer, and cook for 20 to 30 minutes, until tender. Drain.

In a large bowl, whisk together the salt, olive oil, preserved lemon, and lemon juice. Add the warm farro and toss well.

Remove the bottom 2 inches of any thick kale stems. (Do not throw away; see SYS.) Cut the kale into ribbons about ½ inch wide, including the ribs. Add the kale and the apricots to the farro mixture.

Sprinkle the salad with the bread crumbs, if using, just before serving.

Serves 2

2 cups water

¼ teaspoon salt, plus more as needed

1 cup farro

⅓ cup olive oil

¼ preserved lemon (page 95), skin and pulp, minced, seeds removed (about 2 tablespoons)

3 tablespoons fresh lemon juice

1 bunch lacinato kale (Tuscan, black, or dino kale)

¾ cup dried apricots, diced

¼ cup bread crumbs (optional), lightly toasted

SYS
(Save Your Scraps)

Finely chop the kale stems and sneak them into another dish, such as pot pie (page 220), the savory galette (page 212), or the stir-fry (page 181). No one will ever know.

One-Bean, One-Vegetable, One-Grain Salad with Lemon-Garlic Dressing

It's a busy Wednesday night and you're foraging through your refrigerator. You find a jar of cooked chickpeas, some cooked quinoa, one cucumber, and leftover dressing you whipped up on the weekend. In minutes, you can enjoy this filling meal.

You could also make this endlessly versatile dish with black beans, navy beans, borlotti, or adzuki beans; farro or brown rice or buckwheat groats, or that jar of mystery grains in the back of your cupboard; bell peppers, tomatoes, broccoli, avocado, or cooked beets.

If desired, combine the beans, grains, and dressing a day or two ahead. Just before serving, chop up your vegetable of choice and toss it in.

If using dried chickpeas, soak them for 6 hours or longer. Drain and cook according to the directions on page 132 (bean cooking times vary from a few minutes in a pressure cooker to 8 hours in a slow cooker). Drain the cooked chickpeas.

In a jar or small bowl, stir together the lemon juice, garlic, honey, honey mustard, salt, and pepper to taste. Slowly pour in the olive oil and whisk to emulsify. Taste. Adjust the flavor, if necessary. (Can be made in advance and stored in the refrigerator until ready to use.)

Rinse the quinoa. Bring the water to a boil in a medium pot. Add the quinoa and return to a boil, then reduce the heat to medium-low, cover, and simmer until plumped, about 15 minutes. Let rest, covered, for 5 minutes before fluffing with a fork.

In a large bowl, combine the cooked chickpeas, quinoa, and cucumbers. Pour in about ¼ cup of the dressing and toss to coat evenly. Taste. Add more dressing, if desired. Serve immediately.

Serves 2

Scant ½ cup dried chickpeas, or 1 cup cooked chickpeas

3 tablespoons fresh lemon juice

1 garlic clove, minced

½ teaspoon honey or maple syrup

½ teaspoon As You Like It Honey Mustard (page 129) or store-bought

⅛ teaspoon salt, or more as needed

Freshly ground black pepper

¼ cup olive oil

1 cup quinoa

2 cups water or Save-Scraps-Save-Cash Vegetable Broth (page 135)

2 medium cucumbers, cut into bite-size cubes

And now for your next recipe . . .

If you have leftover dressing, make some pesto with it. In a food processor, combine some basil leaves, walnuts, and shredded cheese or nutritional yeast. With the processor running, slowly pour in the dressing, until thickened. Adjust to desired taste and consistency.

Use-All-the-Vegetables Frittata

A frittata satisfies busy cooks and hungry eaters alike. At the end of a long day, the cook can quickly transform humble ingredients on hand into a filling, one-pan dish of savory vegetables suspended in a silky custard that even picky diners will devour. Serve the frittata hot, straight out of the oven, or make it ahead to enjoy later at room temperature.

A 10½-inch cast-iron skillet is the perfect size for this recipe, from start to finish. If you don't have a cast-iron skillet, sauté the vegetables in a stainless-steel skillet (or use whatever type of skillet you have), then assemble the frittata in a glass pie plate to bake in the oven.

Preheat the broiler. Whisk the eggs in a medium bowl with a fork until you no longer see any clear bits of egg white.

Whisk the milk into the eggs and season with salt and pepper.

In a large cast-iron skillet set over medium-high heat, heat the oil and sauté the fresh vegetables for about 5 minutes or until they have released much of their water. Do not skip this step! You want the water released in your pan, not in your eggs. (If using roasted vegetables, just add them to reheat, about 2 minutes.)

Pour the egg-milk mixture over the vegetables in the skillet and cook until the edges begin to set, about 4 minutes.

Transfer the skillet to the broiler and broil for 4 minutes or so, until the center of the omelet is barely set and jiggles like custard. Do not allow it to brown on top; if it browns, you've cooked it a bit too long and risk having a dry frittata.

Serves 4

6 large eggs

½ cup whole milk or half-and-half

Salt and freshly ground black pepper

2 tablespoons olive oil

5 cups fresh vegetables of choice, chopped, or about 4 cups Hearty and Herby Roasted Vegetables (page 176)

And now for your next recipe . . .

Have some leftover frittata made from leftover vegetables? Make a quick sandwich out of it, topped with ketchup (page 126) or kimchi (page 187), or anything else that strikes your fancy! Think of your sandwich as leftovers[2] with exponential deliciousness.

Frugal Fennel-Frond Pesto and Pasta

At my farmers' market, a couple of vendors give away fennel stalks and fronds. Most fennel buyers want the stalks and fronds lopped off, nipping what-on-earth-do-I-do-with-this-stuff guilt in the bulb. So, I get one of the main parts of this pesto for free—the wispy fronds. However, if this cookbook sells so well that it drives up the price of fennel fronds, I apologize.

Although I have no tips on how or where to find flour for free, I can save you a lot of money on expensive tools to make pasta. Homemade pasta *does* turn out beautifully when you run the dough through a pasta machine, but if you don't have one, then a work surface, a knife, and a rolling pin will suffice. And if you have a clean wine bottle, the rolling pin becomes optional, Chef MacGyver.

Make the pesto: Toast the raw nuts in the oven at 350°F for 5 minutes and stir. Toast for another 3 to 5 minutes, until fragrant but not dark.

Place the toasted nuts, garlic, fennel fronds, parsley, and salt in a food processor. Pulse to make a paste. Scrape down the sides of the food processor if necessary.

With the processor running, stream in the oil in a slow trickle, until the pesto is well blended. Transfer to a large serving bowl. (If not using immediately, refrigerate or freeze in a wide-mouth jar.)

Make the pasta: Place the semolina in a large bowl and make a well in the center. Pour in the hot water. (Alternatively, you can make this directly on your work surface. For a beginner, you may prefer to use a bowl.)

With a fork, incorporate the flour from the edges of the well into the water. Continue until you've combined all the flour and water and have formed a crumbly dough.

recipe continues ⟫→

Serves 3

For the Pesto

¼ cup raw nuts, such as walnuts, pecans, almonds, or hazelnuts

2 garlic cloves, smashed

1 cup packed fennel fronds (see Note)

½ cup packed fresh parsley leaves

½ teaspoon salt

¼ cup olive oil

For the Pasta

2½ cups (250 g) durum semolina

¾ cup (125 ml) hot, not boiling, water

1 teaspoon salt

←« recipe continued from previous page

Turn the dough out onto a floured surface. The bowl will likely contain enough unincorporated flour that you won't need more on your work surface. Knead the dough until it is smooth and elastic. It should spring back after you make an indentation in it with your thumb. If it doesn't spring back, keep kneading it. This can take about 10 minutes. Cover with a clean dish towel and let rest for 20 to 30 minutes.

Divide the dough into 2 equal portions; smaller portions are easier to work with. Lightly dust the work surface with semolina, if necessary, as you roll out each piece of the dough to about ⅛ inch thick.

Dust the dough with semolina. Roll each piece of the dough up into a very loose tube (see the picture opposite). You will be slicing noodles from these tubes, so you don't want it too tightly wound and stuck together. Cut ¼-inch-wide noodles from each roll.

Add the salt to a large pot of water and bring to a boil. Add the noodles and cook until tender, about 2 minutes. Reserve at least ⅓ cup of the pasta cooking water. Drain the pasta in a colander.

Whisk the saved pasta cooking water into the bowl with the pesto. Blend and toss the pasta in the pesto and serve.

Note

The pesto recipe works well with kale stems also. Replace the fennel fronds with 1 cup of ½-inch pieces of kale stems.

And now for your next recipe . . .

You now have leftover fennel stalks. Shave them with a vegetable peeler and add them to a salad, such as the bean, vegetable, and grain salad with lemon-garlic dressing (page 206).

Ricotta and Ratatouille Galette

Although ricotta and ratatouille add an appealing alliterative ring to this recipe name, you can make this galette with a variety of vegetables. Sautéed mushrooms, roasted butternut squash, and shallots taste delicious. Caramelized onions, sautéed chard, and thinly sliced potatoes are another option. Let your refrigerator crisper and pantry dictate the filling. For each galette, use about 5 cups of fresh vegetables. By roasting the vegetables first, you'll remove excess moisture that can make the pastry soggy.

Preheat the oven to 400°F.

Place the sliced tomato, bell peppers, eggplant, zucchini, and onion on five separate baking sheets or in cast-iron pans. Drizzle each baking sheet of vegetables with about 1 tablespoon of olive oil, toss with your hands to coat, and spread out the vegetables in single layers. Sprinkle each baking sheet with salt and ¼ teaspoon of the herbes de Provence. (If you don't have enough baking sheets, group the vegetables that bake in a similar amount of time: tomatoes with bell peppers, zucchini with eggplant.)

Roast the vegetables until tender and the edges have begun to brown. They will reach doneness at different times: 15 to 20 minutes for the tomato and bell peppers, 20 to 25 minutes for the zucchini and eggplant, and up to 30 minutes for the onion. Shake the pans or stir the vegetables one time while they cook. Allow the vegetables to cool completely on the baking sheets.

Lower the oven temperature to 375°F if baking the galette right after forming it.

While the vegetables roast, work on the pastry. On a well-floured surface, roll out the pastry to a 14-inch circle, about ⅛ inch thick. Place the dough on a rimmed baking sheet or fit it into a large cast-iron skillet.

Spread the ricotta in the center of the pastry, in a circle about 10 inches in diameter. Leaving a clean 2-inch border around the outer edge of the pastry, layer the roasted vegetables in concentric

Serves 4

1 ripe large tomato, cut into ¼-inch-thick slices

2 medium bell peppers, cored, seeded, and cut into thin strips

1 medium eggplant, cut into ¼-inch-thick half-moons

1 medium zucchini, cut into ¼-inch-thick slices

1 medium white onion, sliced lengthwise

5 tablespoons olive oil

Coarse salt

1¼ teaspoons herbes de Provence

1 recipe No-Fear Pastry (page 107), chilled

1 cup Yes Whey, You Can Make Ricotta (page 117)

2 garlic cloves, sliced thinly

1 large egg, lightly beaten with 1 teaspoon water

circles over the ricotta, alternating the vegetable types and distributing the garlic.

Gently fold the edges of the dough up and a bit over the filling, overlapping as you go, making a border of about 1½ inches wide, leaving most of the vegetables open in the center. Brush the egg wash along the edges of the dough.

Chill the galette in the freezer for 10 minutes (or in the refrigerator for 30 minutes). Then bake for 40 to 50 minutes, until the crust is golden brown. Let cool briefly before serving.

And now for your next recipe . . .

If you have leftover ricotta, add that and the leftover egg wash to the frittata (page 207). If you couldn't fit in all the vegetables you roasted for this galette, or you roasted extra, add those to the frittata as well.

Kernel-to-Cob Corn Chowder

This recipes calls for every part of the corn—the husk, the silk, and the cob for broth and the kernels for the chowder itself. When I consume anything made from the peels or skins of fruits or vegetables, I choose organic produce because the skins and peels usually contain the most pesticide residue. Non-organic sweet corn does contain less pesticide residue than most other fruits and vegetables treated with pesticides, though. In fact, it comes in at second place on EWG's Clean Fifteen List, a ranking of non-organic produce varieties containing the least pesticide residue.

Nevertheless, I would avoid putting silks and husks of non-organic corn into this broth, because they protect the corn kernels from the pesticides that might be used on the crop. But if you can buy organic, the silks and husks really do add flavor.

Like many of the recipes in this book, you can cook this chowder in steps—the broth one day, the soup the next.

Remove the husks and silks from the corn. Scrub the ears well. Use a sharp knife to cut off the kernels.

Place the cobs, husks, and silks in a large pot with 8 cups of water and cover. Bring to a boil over high heat, turn down the heat to medium low, and simmer for 30 to 45 minutes, until the broth turns golden and fragrant and tastes sweet. Strain through a sieve; you'll need approximately 5 cups of broth.

Place 1 cup of the hot broth in a blender and add the cashews; let soak for 10 minutes.

Heat the olive oil over medium heat. Add the garlic, ginger, onion, peppers, and celery and sauté until softened, 5 to 10 minutes. Stir in the oregano. Add the corn kernels and the potatoes, and stir until coated.

Serves 4

4 ears corn on the cob, with husks and silks

8 cups water

½ cup raw cashews

2 tablespoons olive oil

3 garlic cloves, minced

1 (1-inch) piece fresh ginger, minced

1 large onion, chopped

1 to 2 serrano or jalapeño peppers, minced, with seeds

2 celery stalks, including leaves, chopped

1 tablespoon dried oregano

2 small red potatoes, cubed

1 tablespoon fresh lime juice (from 1 lime), or more as needed

1 teaspoon salt, or more as needed

Chopped fresh cilantro

Red pepper flakes (optional), to serve

recipe continues »→

Add 4 cups of the reserved broth, bring to a boil, then cover and turn the heat to medium-low and simmer until the potatoes are tender, about 10 minutes.

Purée the cashews and broth in the blender until creamy.

Add 2 cups of the soup to the blender and purée until smooth, then stir the purée into the pot. Add the lime juice and salt. If desired, add more broth to thin the chowder if it seems too thick. (Refrigerate or freeze any remaining broth.)

Ladle the chowder into bowls and sprinkle with the cilantro and, if desired, the red pepper flakes.

SYS
(Save Your Scraps)

Before you cut and squeeze the lime, zest it. Citrus zest adds so much flavor to food for so little effort, and we mostly throw it away! Freeze or dehydrate your zest and add bits of it to vinaigrettes and salads or to pancakes, waffles, quick breads, and other baked goods.

Cauliflower and Potato Dal

You can't really go wrong with cauliflower, potatoes, and Indian spices. *Dal* (or *dhal*) refers to both the protein-rich lentils and the ubiquitous soupy Indian dish they constitute. I like hearty green lentils in this recipe—they hold up well—but you could use brown, yellow, or black lentils instead. Cooking times can vary with the lentil variety, so check on the pot as it simmers. While the lentils cook, prep everything else and this meal will come together quickly.

In a medium saucepan, combine the lentils and water. Bring to a boil over high heat, then reduce the heat to medium-low, cover, and simmer until barely tender, 20 to 30 minutes. Check the pot and add more water if necessary to ensure the lentils are not going dry.

In a Dutch oven or large pot set over medium heat, heat the olive oil and then add the cumin seeds, stirring constantly for 1 minute, until fragrant. Add the garlic, ginger, onion, and hot peppers, stirring occasionally until the onion is softened, 5 to 10 minutes. Add the turmeric, coriander, and garam masala spices and stir for 1 minute. Add the cauliflower, tomatoes, and potatoes and sauté for 1 minute more.

Stir the lentils and their cooking water into the vegetable mixture. If the mixture isn't just barely covered with liquid, add a little water. Cover and simmer until the potatoes and cauliflower are tender, about 15 minutes.

Stir in the lemon juice, salt, and cilantro. Taste and adjust the seasoning.

Serve with rice or dosas. Garnish with a sprinkling of cilantro and accompany with hot sauce and preserved lemons, if desired.

Serves 4

1 cup dried green lentils

3 cups water

2 tablespoons olive oil

2 teaspoons cumin seeds

4 garlic cloves, minced

1 tablespoon fresh ginger, minced (see Note)

1 medium onion, chopped

1 to 2 jalapeño or serrano peppers, minced (see Note)

1 teaspoon ground turmeric

1 teaspoon ground coriander

1 teaspoon garam masala

2 cups (1-inch) pieces of cauliflower florets

1 pound ripe tomatoes, peeled and chopped (about 2½ cups), or 1 cup roasted tomatoes (page 121)

2 medium Yukon Gold potatoes, chopped into ½-inch pieces

2 tablespoons fresh lemon or lime juice (from 1 lemon or lime), or more as needed (see Note)

1 teaspoon salt, or more as needed

¼ cup chopped fresh cilantro, plus more for garnish

4 cups cooked rice or 12 Indian crepes (dosas; page 182), warmed

Pick-Your-Peppers Hot Sauce (optional; page 91)

Preserved Lemons (optional; page 95)

recipe continues ➻→

← recipe continued from previous page

Notes

- Because I keep a ginger bug going (see page 249), I have lots of fermented minced ginger on my hands. I often use that in this dal in place of fresh ginger.

- Jalapeños tend to add less heat than serranos; I don't seed the hot peppers, which adds more heat.

- Add 2 tablespoons of the juice from the preserved lemons in place of lemon juice for a more complex flavor. Adjust the salt to taste.

And now for your next dish . . .

You likely now have either a partial head of cauliflower on your hands or a bunch of cauliflower florets if you prepped the entire head. Think of this as a kick-starter for a stir-fry (page 181), a pot pie (page 220), or the empamosas with cilantro chutney (see page 184).

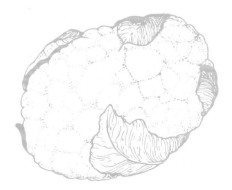

Granny's Pot Pie

We can learn a lot from Granny—how to grow food, how to preserve food, and how to stretch every morsel of food. This kind of thrift, along with Granny's practical skills, helped her survive during the Great Depression. In addition to thriftiness, Granny passed down to her children and grandchildren versatile recipes like this pot pie.

While this recipe works with a variety of vegetables, be generous with the mushrooms as stipulated. They add lots of umami. Granny would have wanted to also remind you to save all the bits and pieces of onions, mushrooms, carrots, and whatnot that you'll accumulate while prepping this vegetable-packed dish. Use those scraps to make the vegetable broth for this pot pie or save them for the next batch of broth.

Preheat the oven to 400°F.

Heat 1 tablespoon of the olive oil in a large skillet or sauté pan over high heat. Add the mushrooms, salt lightly, and stir occasionally until the liquid releases and evaporates, 5 to 8 minutes. Allow the mushrooms to brown. Transfer to a bowl.

Reduce the heat to medium and add the remaining 2 tablespoons oil to the skillet. Add the onion, carrots, celery, and diced vegetables, salt lightly, and sauté until not quite tender, about 5 minutes. Transfer to the bowl with the mushrooms.

Reduce the heat to medium-low and melt the butter in the skillet. Whisk in the flour and cook for 1 minute, then whisk in the broth, followed by the milk.

Bring to a simmer, whisking, until the béchamel is thick and smooth, 2 to 3 minutes. Do not allow the mixture to brown. Off the heat, add the mushrooms and vegetables, then stir in the parsley. Season to taste with salt and pepper.

Transfer the mixture to a 13 by 9-inch baking dish.

Serves 4 to 6

3 tablespoons olive oil

4 cups sliced cremini (brown) mushrooms (about 10 ounces)

Salt and freshly ground black pepper

1 large onion or 3 medium shallots, diced

2 medium carrots, diced

2 celery stalks, including leafy tops, diced

2 cups diced vegetables of choice, such as potatoes, sweet potatoes, squash, pumpkin, Brussels sprouts, parsnips, and turnips

4 tablespoons (½ stick) unsalted butter

½ cup all-purpose flour

2 cups Save-Scraps-Save-Cash Vegetable Broth (page 135)

1½ cups whole milk, half-and-half, or No-Waste Nut or Seed Milk (page 112)

4 tablespoons chopped fresh parsley

1 recipe No-Fear Pastry (page 107), chilled

Roll out the pastry on a floured work surface to a rectangle about 15 by 11 inches and ⅛ inch thick. Wrap it around your rolling pin and drape it across the filling. Tuck in any overhanging dough, nestling it between the filling and the side of the dish. With a sharp knife, slash the top of the pastry several times to make vents for steam to escape while the pie cooks.

Bake until the pastry is golden brown on top and the filling is bubbling up, 25 to 35 minutes.

And now for your next recipe . . .

If you have lots of parsley left over, make some tabbouleh (page 168), a light and refreshing parsley-based salad. It balances nicely with this hearty pot pie.

Chili sans Carne

This recipe provides a good opportunity for me to reiterate that there is more than one way to skin a tomato.

Recipes, such as this chili, serve as a guideline. You are under no moral obligation to char and peel the poblanos. However, charring and peeling the poblanos does enhance the flavor. If desired, you can prep several poblanos at a time to add to other dishes, such as the frittata (page 207), the refried beans (page 180), or even the hummus (page 248). But sometimes you don't have time. Or perhaps you don't like poblanos. Or you can't find them.

As for peeling the tomatoes, in a chunky dish like this, you probably won't notice the skins on fresh tomatoes, if you decide to keep them on. If you use the roasted tomatoes from page 121, you might.

Peeled tomayto, unpeeled tomahto. Like I said, guidelines.

If using dried beans, soak them for at least 6 hours. After soaking, drain and rinse well.

With tongs, place each poblano directly on the rack of a gas burner over a high flame. As one side chars, rotate to char another side. Repeat until the entire poblano has blackened. (Alternatively, heat the oven to 500°F. Place the poblanos in a baking dish or cast-iron skillet and roast for approximately 30 minutes, turning every 10 minutes, until charred on all sides.) Place the charred poblanos in a dish with a lid or in a bowl and place a plate on top. Wait several minutes. The hot poblanos will create steam, which will loosen the skin. Scrape it off with a knife. Seed and chop the peppers. (If desired, prepare the peppers a day or two in advance.)

In a large pot, heat the olive oil over medium heat. Add the onion and garlic and sauté until the onion has softened, 5 to 10 minutes. Add the chili powder, cumin, and oregano and cook, stirring, for 1 minute.

Serves 4

1½ cups dried kidney beans, borlotti beans, black beans, or a combination

2 poblano peppers

2 tablespoons olive oil

1 large onion, diced

4 garlic cloves, minced

1 tablespoon homemade chili powder (page 98) or store-bought

1 tablespoon ground cumin

1 teaspoon dried oregano

2 pounds ripe tomatoes, peeled and chopped (about 4 cups), or 2 cups roasted tomatoes (page 121)

¾ cup bulgur (cracked wheat)

1 teaspoon salt, or more as needed

Juice of 1 lime, or more as needed

¼ cup chopped fresh cilantro

Two-Ingredient Homemade Sour Cream (page 118, optional)

Turn the heat back up to medium. Add the tomatoes and the poblanos. Break up the tomatoes with the back of a wooden spoon. Stir in the beans. Add enough water to just cover. Bring to a boil, reduce the heat to medium low, cover, and simmer for 45 minutes.

Add the bulgur. Continue to cook the chili until the beans are soft and the bulgur is tender, about 15 minutes.

Turn off the heat and stir in the salt and lime juice. Add more as needed. Garnish with the cilantro just before serving and, if desired, spoon on some sour cream.

And now for your next recipe . . .

As with soup, stew, dal, and other aromatic brothy dishes, this chili will taste even better on the second day, after the flavors have melded. So save some chili for your next meal! If you still have chili left, use it as the base filling for the shepherd's pie (page 193)—add a layer of sautéed carrots or other vegetables, top with the mashed potatoes, and, voilà! A whole new dish! Or, cook down the chili until it becomes very thick, and use it to fill hand pies (follow the instructions for the empamosas on page 184).

Ribollita

The Italian word *ribollita* means "reboiled." This soup originated, like so many beloved dishes in the cuisines around the world, from cooks who learned out of necessity how to creatively incorporate every last bit of their food into dishes. In Tuscany, peasants would first make soup from leftover vegetables and, the next day, add dry bread to the pot. They then reboiled the new take on the previous supper.

Before you make the soup, do a quick vegetable inventory. Have a handful of green beans that you couldn't quite squeeze into your jars of dilly beans? Found one lonely parsnip rolling around in your crisper? Not sure how to use the overlooked, yet perfectly edible and tasty bell pepper with a few wrinkles, which still has much to contribute to the world despite what absurd societal expectations dictate? Chop them all up for this soup. In spring, add asparagus. In summer, corn. In fall and winter, squash. Let the seasons determine the menu.

If you'd like to eat two slightly different variations on this soup, omit the bread the first night. The next night, add the bread to the pot but less than the recipe calls for, as you'll now have less liquid for the bread to absorb.

If using dried beans, soak them for at least 6 hours. Drain and rinse well.

Heat the olive oil in a large stockpot over medium heat. Add the onions, garlic, and red pepper flakes. Sauté until the onions have softened, 5 to 10 minutes. Increase the heat to medium and stir in the tomatoes, breaking them up with the back of a wooden spoon.

Stir the rosemary, thyme, bay leaves, dried beans, 3 quarts of the broth, and the cheese rinds (if using) into the pot. Bring to a boil, reduce the heat to medium-low, cover, and simmer until the beans are tender, about 1 hour.

recipe continues »→

Serves 8

2 cups dried borlotti, cannellini, or pinto beans, or 5 to 6 cups cooked beans

½ cup olive oil

4 medium onions, finely chopped

8 garlic cloves, minced

½ to 1 teaspoon red pepper flakes

4 pounds ripe tomatoes, peeled and chopped (about 8 cups), or 4 cups roasted tomatoes (page 121)

2 sprigs fresh rosemary, leaves stripped and chopped

2 sprigs fresh thyme, leaves stripped and chopped

2 bay leaves

3 to 4 quarts Save-Scraps-Save-Cash Vegetable Broth (page 135), leftover whey from making ricotta (see page 117), water, or a combination

2 cheese rinds (optional)

4 celery stalks, including leafy tops, chopped

4 medium carrots, chopped

1 pound savoy cabbage, cored and chopped

1 pound lacinato kale (Tuscan, black, or dino kale)

2 teaspoons salt, or more as needed

1 teaspoon freshly ground black pepper, or more as needed

10 to 12 cups (2-inch) pieces stale hearty bread

Grated cheese of choice, for serving (optional)

←« recipe continued from previous page

Stir in the celery, carrots, cabbage, and kale (and any other vegetables you're using). If using cooked beans, add them now. Simmer for about 30 minutes.

Remove the bay leaves and cheese rinds, if used. Add the salt and pepper, taste, and adjust the seasonings as needed.

Just before serving, add the stale bread. It will sop up the delicious broth and thicken it. If desired, add some or all of the remaining 4 cups broth to thin the soup to preferred consistency.

Top with freshly grated cheese, if desired.

SYS
(Save Your Scraps)

If you have leftover fresh rosemary or thyme sprigs, or both, dry them. Wash and dry the herbs thoroughly. Tie the sprigs together with string or kitchen twine—one bundle of each type—and hang them upside down in a dark, dry place, such as a cupboard. After 7 to 10 days, the leaves will become dry and brittle. Transfer them to a jar for long-term storage. Crush just before using.

Sourdough Pizza
with Tomato-Garlic Sauce

I've been making pizza since my now-grown kids were tiny. I've made it with commercial yeast, discarded sourdough starter, and active sourdough starter. This chewy, naturally leavened, air-pocket-filled sourdough crust is by far our favorite. As with sourdough bread, the magic of fermentation coaxes incredible flavor from the three basic ingredients: flour, water, and salt.

——————————— Day 1 ◦ 8 a.m. ———————————

Make the leaven: Combine the flours, water, and starter in a jar or non-reactive bowl, mix well, and cover with a lid or plate. Set aside at room temperature until the leaven has approximately doubled in size.

——————————— Day 1 ◦ 2 p.m. or later ———————————

1. Make the dough: In a large, non-reactive bowl, combine the flours and salt. Stir in the warm water and mix as well as you can with a fork. The dough will be very stiff.

2. Stir down the leaven to remove the air bubbles. With a wet hand, mix the leaven into the dough.

3. Turn the shaggy dough out onto a floured surface and knead for about 3 minutes to shape it into a ball. Place the dough back in the bowl and cover with a thin cloth. Note the time. This is the beginning of the bulk fermentation, which will last approximately 3 hours.

4. After 45 minutes, do the first set of stretches and folds of the dough. With a wet hand, reach underneath the bottom of the dough, pull the dough up, and fold it over onto itself. Turn the

recipe continues »→

Makes three 10-inch pizzas

For the Leaven

2 tablespoons (18 g) all-purpose flour

2 tablespoons (18 g) whole wheat flour

Generous 2 tablespoons (36 ml) water

1 tablespoon (16 g) active sourdough starter (see page 105)

For the Dough

4 cups (525 g) all-purpose flour

½ cup (60 g) whole wheat flour

1 tablespoon (15 g) coarse salt

1⅔ cups (380 ml) warm water

Olive oil, for greasing

For the Tomato-Garlic Sauce

⅜ cup olive oil

4 garlic cloves, minced

4 ripe medium tomatoes, chopped (about 3 cups)

1 teaspoon dried oregano

1 teaspoon dried basil

1 teaspoon salt

Freshly ground black pepper

Optional Toppings

Caramelized onions, sautéed mushrooms, chopped bell peppers, cherry tomatoes, fresh basil leaves, arugula, shredded cheese, crumbled feta cheese bowl a quarter turn and repeat the stretching and folding. Repeat 2 more times, for a total of 4 turns. (See the picture on page 145 of stretching sourdough bread dough; the pizza dough is much stiffer, but it follows the same general method.)

5. Repeat this 4-turn stretching and folding about once an hour during the 3-hour bulk fermentation. If the dough becomes too stiff to do the final set of stretches and folds, let it rest for the remainder of the bulk fermentation.

——————————— Day 1 • 5:15 p.m. ———————————

1. Turn out the dough onto the lightly floured surface. With your wet hands, rotate the dough gently while pushing the sides toward the bottom until you have a fairly uniform ball of dough. Don't overwork the dough.

2. Grease the bowl with olive oil and place the dough back in the bowl. Turn the dough over so the slightly oiled bottom faces up. Cover with a plate and refrigerate overnight or for up to 24 hours.

——————————— Day 2 • 12 p.m. ———————————

1. Grease a 9 by 13-inch glass baking dish.

2. Turn out the dough onto a very lightly floured work surface. Divide the dough into 3 pieces.

3. Roll each piece into a ball. Hold the ball in your hands, pulling the sides down with both thumbs toward its bottom. Rotate and continue to pull down the sides and pinch the dough until you have formed a smooth ball, pinching the bottoms together as you rotate. Flatten the ball slightly.

4. Place the dough balls in the baking dish, spaced evenly apart. Very lightly coat each ball with a bit of olive oil to prevent the tops from drying out. Cover the baking dish with an inverted cookie sheet or damp towel and allow the balls to rise at room temperature for about 4 to 5 hours or until smooth and puffy.

recipe continues ⟶

—————————————— Day 2 ∘ 4:30 p.m. ——————————————

1. Place a pizza stone in the oven. (Alternatively, you can bake the pizzas in a large cast-iron pan or on a baking sheet sprinkled with cornmeal.) Preheat the oven to 500°F.

2. Make the sauce: Heat the olive oil in a large skillet over medium heat. Sauté the garlic until fragrant, about 1 minute. Add the tomatoes, oregano, basil, salt, and pepper. Lower the heat to medium-low, and simmer, uncovered, breaking up the tomatoes with the back of a wooden spoon and stirring until thickened, about 20 minutes.

3. Pour the sauce into a blender or food processor, if desired, for a smoother sauce. (Sauce can be made a day or so ahead.)

4. Using a dough scraper, transfer 1 dough ball to the floured work surface. Flatten the dough into a disk with your hands. Lift the disk up on one edge and let gravity stretch it down. Rotate it several times, letting it stretch itself until you have a 10-inch flat round of dough.

5. Sprinkle a little flour on a wooden pizza peel, then place the dough round on it. (Alternatively, use a medium cutting board.) Working quickly to prevent the pizza from sticking, spread about ¼ cup of sauce (or more, if desired) on the dough. Top with vegetables and cheeses of choice.

6. Give the pizza peel a quick jerk to make sure the pizza will slide off. If the dough sticks, lift it up at one edge and spread more flour underneath. Open the oven door and tilt the pizza peel at an angle over the pizza stone, near the back. As the pizza slides off the peel, pull the pizza peel out quickly from beneath the pizza.

7. Bake for 7 minutes, after which turn the oven to broil and broil for 1 minute.

While the pizza bakes, form the other two dough balls into rounds.

And now for your next recipe . . .

If you have pizza sauce left, use it to top baked potatoes, along with other favorite pizza toppings, or stir it into a pot of chili or a tomato-based soup.

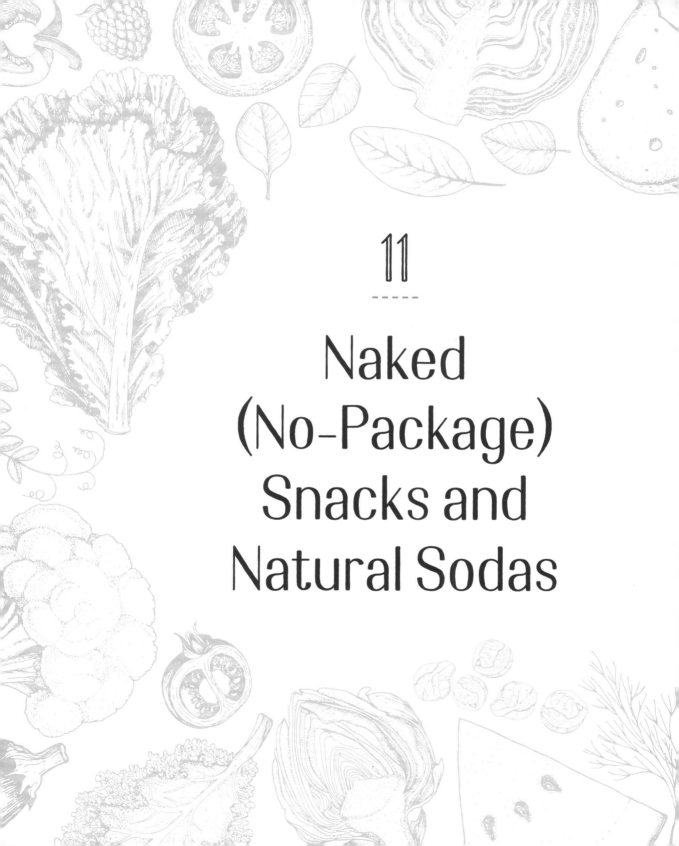

11

Naked (No-Package) Snacks and Natural Sodas

Sourdough Crackers with Everything-Bagel Seasoning

If you want to make a dent in the discarded starter stashed away in your refrigerator, bake a batch or two of these crunchy, addictive crackers. They taste cheesy but contain no cheese. Rather, that tang comes from the discarded starter. As the bacteria and yeast continue to eat the remaining sugars in the flour, they create more acids and the starter becomes more sour and tangy.

The everything-bagel seasoning goes perfectly with these crackers, but they also taste delicious with only a sprinkling of salt on top before baking.

Make the seasoning: Combine the salt, white and black sesame seeds, poppy seeds, garlic, and onion in a small bowl.

Make the dough: In a large non-reactive bowl, combine the sourdough starter and oil. In a medium bowl, combine the flour, salt, and baking soda. Add the dry ingredients to the bowl with the wet ingredients and mix. If necessary, knead the dough a few times to incorporate the last bit of flour. If the dough is very sticky, add 1 to 2 more tablespoons of flour.

Cover the bowl with a plate and let the dough ferment for up to 6 hours at room temperature (see note). Chill the dough for 30 minutes. (If not baking right away, store the dough in the refrigerator for up to 5 days. When ready to use, warm it at room temperature for 15 minutes to make rolling easier.)

Preheat the oven to 350°F.

Divide the dough into two halves on a generously floured surface.

Makes 30 crackers

For the Seasoning

1½ teaspoons flaked or coarse salt

2 teaspoons white sesame seeds

1¾ teaspoons black sesame seeds

1 teaspoon poppy seeds

2 teaspoons dried minced garlic

1¾ teaspoons dried minced onion

For the Dough

⅔ cup (187 g) discarded sourdough starter (see page 105), stirred down

3 heaping tablespoons (40 ml) olive oil or melted coconut oil

¾ cup (100 g) whole wheat flour, plus more as needed

¼ teaspoon salt

¼ teaspoon baking soda

recipe continues ⟫→

Begin to roll out one of the dough halves. If necessary, sprinkle with flour between rollings to prevent the dough from sticking to your work surface. Roll it out to a thickness of about $\frac{1}{16}$ inch, but before completing your final couple of rolls, lift the dough up and sprinkle half the bagel seasoning onto the work surface. Place the dough on top of the seasoning and roll to $\frac{1}{16}$-inch thickness, making the seasoning mix stick to the bottom of the dough. Transfer the dough to an ungreased baking sheet, seasoning side up.

Repeat with the other dough half, and place it on another ungreased baking sheet.

Cut the dough pieces into rectangles with a pastry wheel, pizza cutter, or butter knife. Bake for 8 minutes, then rotate the baking sheets, and bake for an additional 5 to 8 minutes. The crackers are done when crispy and slightly browned.

Transfer the crackers to a rack to cool. (Crackers can be stored in a glass jar for at least 1 week. They also freeze well.)

Note

If desired, skip the fermentation step.

And now for your next recipe . . .

You'll find many uses for this everything-bagel seasoning, so you might want to double or even triple the recipe. Sprinkle it on top of roasted vegetables (page 176), the frittata (page 207), or hummus (page 248) that you've spread on a piece of sourdough toast.

Savory Spiced Nuts

If you made the Grown-Up Brownies (page 263) or the lemon or lime curd (page 138) and now have leftover egg whites, quickly whip up a batch of these crunchy and savory spiced nuts. Use almonds only or add macadamia nuts or walnuts or peanuts, or a combination of nuts. Or change up the spices: Sprinkle in a teaspoon of garlic granules, omit the red pepper flakes, or add some of the homemade chili powder (page 98). The combinations are endless. The spices I've included here add a mild amount of heat.

Preheat the oven to 300°F. Lightly oil a baking sheet.

In a medium bowl, whisk the egg white until frothy. Stir in the cumin, coriander, cayenne, red pepper flakes, and salt. Add the nuts and stir to coat evenly.

Spread the nuts in a single layer on the baking sheet. Bake for 15 minutes, then stir to break up the clumps. Bake another 10 to 12 minutes, until the nuts are browned and have a nice crunch.

Break up any nuts that stick together. Eat immediately or allow to cool completely before storing in glass jars. The nuts will keep for at least 1 week.

Makes 3 cups

1 egg white

1 teaspoon ground cumin

1 teaspoon ground coriander

½ teaspoon cayenne pepper

½ teaspoon red pepper flakes

2 teaspoons salt

1 cup raw almonds

1 cup raw cashews

1 cup raw pecans

And now for your next recipe . . .

If you don't finish off all these spiced nuts by the handful, chop them and sprinkle on top of a salad to add a satisfying crunch.

Crispy Roasted Chickpeas
with Herbes de Provence

Typically, some essence of what I cook for one night's dinner—the broth left behind from cooking beans, the seeds from inside a roasted pumpkin, or the pesto I prepared to swirl into soup—carries over to the next day's meal. I'll call this Buddhist cooking.

If you cook dried chickpeas for the takeout-style chana masala (page 197), for example, you may as well cook extra since you are going to the trouble. After you polish off the chana masala, use some of those extra chickpeas to whip up a batch of preserved lemon hummus (page 248). Or, toss a cup of the chickpeas into a salad the next night, or add them to the Feed-the-Flock Bean and Mushroom Shepherd's Pie (page 193). In your chickpeas' final incarnation, roast them in olive oil, seasonings, and a bit of salt, at which point they will have reached chickpea nirvana.

This recipe calls for herbes de Provence, a blend of dried thyme, rosemary, basil, savory, fennel, and other herbs, such as lavender. Look for good-quality herbes de Provence or make a blend yourself. The herbs make all the difference here. Roasted chickpeas also taste delicious with the nacho cheese seasoning for popcorn on page 247 or the spiced nuts seasoning on page 239.

If using dried chickpeas, soak them for at least 6 hours. Drain and cook according to directions on page 132 (bean cooking times vary from a few minutes in a pressure cooker to 8 hours in a slow cooker). Drain and rinse the chickpeas. Rub the chickpeas in a clean kitchen towel until they are very dry. Remove any skins that peel off.

Preheat the oven to 400°F. Lightly grease a rimmed baking sheet.

Spread the chickpeas in a single layer on the baking sheet. Give the sheet a few shakes to evenly distribute them.

Makes about 2 cups

1 cup dried chickpeas, or 3 cups cooked chickpeas

2 tablespoons olive oil, plus more to grease the baking sheet

1 tablespoon herbes de Provence

½ teaspoon salt

recipe continues ⟶

←« recipe continued from previous page

Bake for 15 minutes.

In a large bowl, combine the olive oil, herbes de Provence, and salt.

Carefully transfer the hot chickpeas to the bowl with the oil and spices, and toss to coat evenly.

Return the chickpeas to the baking sheet and roast 10 to 15 minutes longer, until the chickpeas have turned crunchy and have a rich, golden brown color.

These taste best immediately after roasting. (If you have leftovers, however, transfer them to a jar and store at room temperature.)

And now for your next recipe . . .

You'll probably eat all of these straight out of the oven. However, if some survive, toss them into the farro and kale salad (page 204) or add them to roasted vegetables (page 176) at the end of roasting.

Thin and Crunchy
Granola Bars

Enjoy better-tasting granola bars while eliminating all the single-use plastic packaging of individually wrapped bars.

When I bake these granola bars, I grease and flour the baking dish well before pressing in the granola mixture so it doesn't stick. Now, because this is a zero-waste cookbook—with the goal of throwing nothing away—I can't tell you to line your 9 by 13-inch baking dish with a piece of compostable, unbleached parchment paper in order to prevent the granola bars from sticking. And if you use this parchment paper that I am not recommending, you can reuse the piece several times before composting it.

Preheat the oven to 300°F. Grease a 9 by 13-inch glass baking dish or metal pan with a little olive oil. Sprinkle on a little flour and shake and tilt the dish to distribute evenly. (Alternatively, line the baking dish with parchment paper.)

Place ½ cup of the oats in a food processor and process for about 30 seconds to render a very coarse oat flour.

Combine the remaining 1¼ cups oats with the coconut, sunflower seeds, mixed nuts, and salt in a large bowl.

In a smaller bowl, whisk together the olive oil, nut butter, maple syrup, and vanilla. Stir in the ground oats, then add the dates.

Stir the wet ingredients into the dry ingredients. Use your hands to incorporate everything well.

Transfer the granola mixture to the baking dish. With a dampened hand, press the mixture very firmly into the corners of the dish until you have a thin, even layer. Flatten with the bottom of a metal measuring cup. Bake for 15 minutes. Rotate the dish and continue to bake for another 10 minutes, or until golden around the edges.

Cool completely, then cut into bars and remove from the pan. (Store in a glass jar or container at room temperature, for at least 5 days.)

Makes 12 bars

1 tablespoon olive oil, plus extra to grease the baking dish

Flour, for dusting the baking dish

1¾ cups old-fashioned rolled oats

⅔ cup unsweetened shredded coconut

½ cup sunflower seeds

½ cup chopped mixed nuts

¼ teaspoon salt

2 tablespoons Any-Nut Nut Butter (page 130) or store-bought

¼ cup plus 1 tablespoon maple syrup

¼ teaspoon Bourbon Street Vanilla Extract (page 110) or store-bought

¾ cup chopped pitted dates (from 7 or 8 dates)

And now for your next recipe . . .

If you somehow have any granola bars left, break them up and add to any granola-friendly dish—layer in a fruit and yogurt parfait, toss into a salad, or sprinkle on top of hot baked sweet potatoes.

Give Me S'more Sourdough Graham Crackers

Crunchy, slightly sweet, and with a grainy texture, these homemade graham crackers taste better than anything you can buy in a box.

Graham flour contains the most nutritious parts of the grain—the germ and the bran. If you can't find graham flour, combine ⅔ cup all-purpose flour with a scant ⅓ cup wheat bran and 1½ teaspoons wheat germ. And if you've run out of brown sugar, you can "make" that, too! Simply mix a couple teaspoons of molasses with a cup of granulated sugar. Use what you need, and store the rest in a jar in the cupboard.

Make the leaven: Between 6 and 12 hours before you make the cracker dough, combine the flours, water, and starter in a jar or non-reactive bowl, mix well, cover with a lid or plate, and set aside at room temperature.

Make the crackers: In a large bowl, combine the melted butter and honey with the leaven.

In a medium bowl, combine the graham flour, whole wheat flour, salt, baking soda, cinnamon, and brown sugar.

Add the dry ingredients to the wet ingredients and mix until combined. Knead the dough a few times in the bowl to incorporate everything, then cover the bowl with a plate and refrigerate for at least 1 hour.

Remove the dough from the refrigerator and let warm up at room temperature for about 15 minutes.

Preheat the oven to 350°F. Lightly grease 2 large baking sheets with a little butter.

Makes 24 crackers

For the Leaven

¼ cup (30 g) all-purpose flour

¼ cup (30 g) whole wheat or spelt flour

¼ cup (60 g) water

2 tablespoons (30 g) active sourdough starter (page 105)

For the Crackers

3 tablespoons (43 g) unsalted butter, melted, plus additional for greasing the baking sheets

2 tablespoons (42 g) honey

1 cup (120 g) graham flour, plus more as needed

2 tablespoons (17 g) whole wheat or spelt flour

¼ teaspoon salt

¼ teaspoon baking soda

¼ teaspoon ground cinnamon

¼ cup (49 g) brown sugar

Divide the dough into two halves on a generously floured surface. Roll each dough half out into rectangles that are $\frac{1}{16}$ to $\frac{1}{8}$ inch thick. Lightly sprinkle a little flour on your work surface as needed to prevent the dough from sticking.

Transfer the dough halves to the baking sheets. Cut each rectangle into smaller 1 by 2-inch rectangles with a pastry wheel, pizza cutter, or knife. Poke holes in the dough with a fork.

Bake for 8 minutes, then rotate the baking sheets, and bake until the crackers are barely browned, 5 to 8 minutes more. Transfer the crackers to a rack to cool, where they will crisp up. Store the cooled crackers in a glass jar or container. They will keep for at least 5 days at room temperature or for several months in the freezer.

And now for your next recipe . . .

This cookbook contains recipes for all the components of a simple, cheesecake-like dessert. Spread 3 to 4 crushed sourdough graham crackers in the bottom of an 8-ounce dessert dish, add ¼ cup labneh (see page 115), and top with 2 to 3 tablespoons of quick berry pancake and waffle sauce (page 153).

Stovetop Popcorn
with Nacho Cheese Seasoning

Popcorn is a zero-waste food group. Because once you've banned the plastic packages from your kitchen, you've essentially banned chips and cheese puffs, and microwave popcorn as well. These kinds of self-imposed embargoes may sound like a hardship, but they actually lead to much better-tasting, much less expensive, much healthier food—and much more stovetop-popped popcorn.

If you peeled tomatoes for chana masala (page 197) or the ribolitta (page 225) and saved the skins to avert a bout of zero-waste guilt syndrome (ZWGS), you've found your antidote! Dehydrate the tomato skins, then grind them in a spice grinder and add the remaining spices for waste-not, want-more popcorn with a cheesy topping reminiscent of a certain snack food that rhymes with *mojito*.

Stove-top popcorn also tastes delicious with only salt. If you omit the seasoning, add salt directly to the pot when popping.

In a spice mill or small-capacity blender, combine the ground tomato skins, nutritional yeast, salt, garlic, onion, cumin, chili powder, turmeric, and hot pepper ribs and seeds, if using. Grind, scraping the sides as necessary, and continue to process until everything is blended well.

Place the oil and popcorn kernels in a large pot, place the lid on top, and turn the heat to high. Shake the pot almost constantly. When the kernels begin to pop, they will finish popping in only another minute or two.

Immediately pour the popped corn into a bowl large enough to toss it well. Sprinkle on 3 to 4 tablespoons of the seasoning, or to taste, and toss until evenly coated.

And now for your next recipe . . .

Unless you popped another pot of popcorn, you now have extra seasoning. Add it to the spiced nuts (page 239) or the roasted chickpeas (page 240).

Serves 3

1 tablespoon ground dehydrated tomato skins (see Note)

3 tablespoons nutritional yeast

1½ teaspoons salt

1 teaspoon granulated garlic

1 teaspoon granulated onion

1 teaspoon ground cumin

½ teaspoon homemade chili powder (page 98) or store-bought

½ teaspoon ground turmeric

Ribs and seeds of 1 serrano pepper (optional)

2 tablespoons coconut oil, melted, or 1 tablespoon melted coconut oil and 1 tablespoon olive oil

½ cup popcorn kernels

Note

To dehydrate the tomato skins, preheat the oven to 200°F. Spread the skins out in a single layer on a cooling rack set on top of a baking sheet. Bake the skins for 2 hours, or until completely dried out. After the tomato skins have cooled, grind them in a spice mill or small capacity blender. (To save time, dehydrate many tomato peels at once and store the ground peels in a jar alongside your other spices.)

Preserved Lemon Hummus

As you reduce your household waste, your intake of hummus becomes inversely proportionate: The less waste you produce, the more hummus you eat. It's a bit of a chicken-and-egg riddle: Does your waste decrease because you eat so much hummus, or does your hummus intake increase because you reduce your waste? As my strict Catholic mother taught me, we are not meant to understand some mysteries.

If using dried chickpeas, soak them for at least 6 hours. Drain and cook according to the directions on page 132. Drain and separately reserve the chickpeas and the cooking liquid.

Place the chickpeas, tahini, olive oil, garlic, preserved lemon, juice from the jar of preserved lemons, fresh lemon juice, cumin, cayenne, and ¾ teaspoon salt in a food processor and process until smooth.

Add between 2 and 4 tablespoons of the chickpea liquid to thin the hummus, 1 tablespoon at a time, until desired thickness. Check seasonings and then serve. Store leftovers in the refrigerator. The hummus will keep for at least 1 week.

Makes 3 cups

1 cup dried chickpeas; or 3 cups cooked chickpeas, with liquid

2 tablespoons tahini

2 tablespoons olive oil

2 garlic cloves

½ preserved lemon (page 95), seeds removed

2 tablespoons preserved lemon juice

3 tablespoons fresh lemon juice

1 teaspoon ground cumin

⅛ to ¼ teaspoon cayenne pepper

¾ teaspoon salt, or more as needed

And now for your next recipe . . .

Thin out leftover hummus with some olive oil, a bit of lemon juice, and a bit of the cooking liquid or water for a chickpea salad dressing. Toss with chopped cucumbers, tomatoes, bell peppers, red onion, or other vegetables.

Ginger Bug

A ginger bug—which requires only ginger, sugar, and water (and time)—is a starter culture that can ferment a variety of naturally carbonated drinks, such as Spicy Ginger Beer (page 252). Unlike with kombucha (see page 255), for which you need to track down a living culture that will brew your drinks, you *make* a living culture when you create a ginger bug. Let me explain: When you make a ginger bug, you nurture the bacteria and yeasts present on the fresh ginger (and on your hands and in the air), supporting the starter culture as it develops, sort of like a midwife for microbes. Once the ginger bug gestation period has ended—only about five days— your cute little bug will be ready to ferment delicious, natural sodas. They grow up so quickly!

Before you start, please take note! Be sure to use organic ginger in this recipe. Of all the fermented foods I've made, only one failed to spring to life—pickled ginger. I read later in Sandor Katz's *The Art of Fermentation* that non-organic ginger may have been irradiated, which kills the bacteria and yeast. I've stuck with organic ginger since then, with no problems.

Place the ginger and sugar in a clean glass jar. Add the water and stir vigorously. Cover the jar with a small breathable cloth and secure it with either a string or a rubber band to let air in and keep impurities out. Avoid flimsy cheesecloth and choose something with a tighter weave. Set the jar aside at room temperature. Feed the ginger bug daily for 5 days, adding 1 tablespoon ginger and 1 tablespoon sugar each day. Stir vigorously after adding.

Your bug will bubble and smell yeasty, and have a cloudy yellow color with some ginger floating on the surface and white yeast settled on the bottom. If your kitchen is cold, this might take longer. Be patient!

Makes 1½ cups

To Start
1 tablespoon grated or finely minced organic ginger, peeled or unpeeled

1 tablespoon granulated sugar

1½ cups water

To Feed Daily
1 tablespoon grated or minced organic ginger, peeled or unpeeled

1 tablespoon granulated sugar

recipe continues »→

←◀◀ recipe continued from previous page

When you are ready to use the ginger bug, strain out the amount you need (e.g., ½ cup). After removing the liquid, add to the jar the equivalent amount in water and continue to feed the bug its daily meal of ginger and sugar.

When you strain out some liquid, also remove a couple spoonfuls of the ginger bits to keep the volume in the jar manageable. Use these bits in recipes calling for minced ginger. You can also freeze them.

Once you have established your ginger bug, you can keep it on the kitchen counter, but you must continue to feed it daily. At this point, though, you can remove the cloth and close the jar with a lid, if desired.

If you want a break from the feedings, place the closed jar in the refrigerator. Once a week, take your ginger bug out of the refrigerator, bring it to room temperature, feed it its ginger and sugar, let it sit for an hour or two at room temperature, and then put it back in the refrigerator—unless you want to make a drink!

A regularly fed ginger bug will continue to make fermented drinks for several months. Eventually, however, it may begin to taste alcoholic. At this point, start a new ginger bug.

And now for your next recipe . . .

You'll likely want to make the spicy ginger beer (page 252). You can also use your ginger bug to ferment sweetened herbal tea or juice. Add ¼ to ½ cup strained ginger bug liquid to 4 cups sweetened herbal tea or juice. Pour into bottles, let sit at room temperature for 2 days or longer, and then move to the refrigerator to stop the fermentation. Burp (i.e., open) the bottles every 2 days at least to release pressure from carbon dioxide building in the bottles.

Spicy Ginger Beer

Ginger beer tastes like grown up ginger-ale with a spicy kick that burns the back of your throat in a pleasant way. Although all fermented foods contain at least some alcohol, if you stop the fermentation early (after two to three days), the ginger beer will contain a negligible amount of alcohol, *generally* (see Note). I like to ferment my ginger beer for a week to ten days—sometimes longer, in which case it definitely contains alcohol but still not as much as a bottle of beer.

To make ginger beer, you first need to make a ginger bug (page 249), the starter that will ferment your drink and transform ordinary ingredients into spicy bubbly goodness.

My ginger beer tends to be extremely carbonated. If you don't have any flip-top bottles with tight seals, jars with tight-fitting lids, such as mason jars, may suffice to carbonate your drink while it ferments. Whether you use flip-top bottles, screw-top bottles, or mason jars, be sure to "burp" your ginger beer every day or two to release pressure building up inside.

Keep the following ratio in mind to increase or decrease the yield: 1 cup sugar : 8 cups ginger water : ½ to 1 cup ginger bug liquid.

Place the ginger and water in a medium pot. Bring to a boil over high heat, turn down the heat to medium-low, and simmer for about 15 minutes.

While the ginger simmers, stir your ginger bug, being sure to incorporate the white residue at the bottom of the jar; you want this yeast in your drink. Strain out ½ to 1 cup liquid from your ginger bug. Depending on your kitchen environment and the vigor of your ginger bug, ½ cup may suffice and brew a very carbonated drink.

Strain out the simmered ginger pieces and retain the ginger water; you will have approximately half the liquid you started out with.

Makes 9 to 10 cups

1 (6-inch) piece organic ginger (about 4 ounces), peeled if desired, cut into ⅛-inch slices

3 cups water

½ to 1 cup strained liquid from Ginger Bug (page 249)

1 cup sugar

1 cup fresh lemon juice (optional)

In a large bowl, preferably with a spout for easy pouring, combine the sugar with the ginger water, stirring until the sugar dissolves. Add between 6 and 7 cups of room-temperature water to the bowl so as to have 8 cups liquid. Let the mixture cool completely; heat will kill your microbes in the ginger bug and your ginger beer won't ferment.

Add the liquid from your ginger bug. Add the lemon juice, if using.

Using a funnel, pour the mixture into clean, flip-top bottles and close them. Set them aside at room temperature for 2 to 3 days and up to 10 days. The longer you ferment the ginger beer, the less sweet it will taste. Every day or two, release some of the carbon dioxide building up inside the bottles by burping them (i.e., open them slightly). If, when opening the bottles, you don't hear much of a hiss or feel pressure on the lid, burp the bottles less frequently. (Too-frequent burping will release so much carbon dioxide that no carbonation builds up. On the other hand, if your drink begins to spray the ceiling, try to close it and burp more frequently. Too much carbon dioxide risks exploding bottles.) If you have a cool garage, store them there in a cardboard box to contain any explosions. I have never had a bottle explode, but it can happen, so I store my bottles in a cupboard.

Transfer the bottles to the refrigerator to chill when you are ready to drink the ginger beer. It will keep in the refrigerator for many months, however, the bacteria and yeast will continue to slowly eat the sugars, further reducing the sweetness in the drink and increasing the carbonation. If you leave the bottles in the refrigerator, burp them every 2 weeks.

Note

If you make ginger beer in your boiler room of a kitchen during a drippingly humid Floridian summer with temperatures reaching triple digits, your drink will ferment very quickly and turn alcoholic before you have a chance to move it to the refrigerator to slow down the fermentation.

And now for your next recipe . . .

You'll find several uses for the grated bits of ginger that you remove from your ginger bug when you strain out the liquid for this ginger beer. I use these little bits in recipes that call for minced ginger, such as the empamosas with cilantro chutney (page 184), the cauliflower and potato dal (page 217), or the peanut sauce stir-fry (page 181). This speeds up your prep and uses up your ginger.

Lemon Zesty Kombucha

If you can brew a pot of tea, you possess the requisite skills to brew kombucha, a naturally fermented tea with living cultures, currently undergoing a renaissance, like so many other fermented foods. But to brew your kombucha, you'll have to hunt down the SCOBY, or symbiotic culture of bacteria and yeast, which ferments the tea.

To get a SCOBY, search on Craigslist, Nextdoor, your local Buy Nothing Group, or Facebook Marketplace. The borderline irresponsible way kombucha SCOBYs reproduce, you may find someone desperate to unload a few layers of SCOBY onto you. Also, you can attempt to make a SCOBY. Buy a bottle of unflavored, good-quality raw kombucha, pour a few inches into a wide-mouth jar, and cover securely with a cloth that allows air to circulate. A thin SCOBY *may* begin to form on top after about a week. Once it's about ¼ inch thick, use it to brew kombucha. Or, you could order a SCOBY online from Kombucha Kamp (kombuchakamp.com) or search for one on Etsy (etsy.com).

Once you have your hands on a SCOBY, brew tea from the *Camelia sinensis* plant—black, green, oolong, white, or puerh. Do not use herbal tea or tea with oils, such as Earl Grey with bergamot, or with flavorings such as vanilla—your SCOBY may not agree with these and die. Your SCOBY may like honey or agave, or it may not, and it will downright despise stevia. When you just start out, use real sugar to sweeten the tea; the sugar feeds the bacteria and yeasts in the SCOBY. Once your SCOBYs have reproduced, you can experiment with different sweeteners, if you'd like. Should anything go wrong, you'll have backup SCOBYs.

When your kombucha is ready to drink in a week or two, you can flavor it and bottle it to build up carbonation. You'll need two 16-ounce bottles (or one 32-ounce bottle) for the four cups of kombucha this recipe yields. The tight seals of flip-top bottles work best for building up the carbonation.

This recipe calls for a flavoring from an often overlooked ingredient—lemon zest. I almost always have a little stash of lemon zest in the freezer. You can also flavor your kombucha with fresh fruit, fruit juice, or herbs. Experiment with different combinations. This recipe is based on Sandor Katz's recipe in *The Art of Fermentation*.

Makes two 16-ounce bottles

1 heaping tablespoon loose leaf tea (black, green, oolong, white, puerh, or a combination)

1 cup boiling water

½ cup granulated sugar, sucanat, rapadura, or coconut sugar

3 to 4 cups room-temperature water

½ cup kombucha from a previous batch, or 2 tablespoons raw apple cider vinegar with live mother (such as Braggs brand)

1 SCOBY

2 teaspoons lemon zest

recipe continues »»→

←« recipe continued from previous page

Fill a tea ball or infuser with the loose tea. Place it in a pot, teapot, or Pyrex measuring cup and pour in the boiling water. After the tea turns very dark and strong, remove the tea ball. Add the sugar and stir to dissolve.

Pour the room-temperature water into a large wide-mouth jar that can hold 6 to 8 cups of liquid. Stir in the sweetened tea.

When the tea has cooled to room temperature, stir in the fermented kombucha. This inoculates your tea from bad bacteria and mold. (Caution: Do not add live cultures to hot tea or the heat will kill them and your kombucha may not ferment.)

Gently drop your SCOBY into your jar. It should float to the surface but may sink initially. (Again, never add the SCOBY to hot tea.) To prevent impurities from finding their way into the jar, cover it with a breathable, tightly woven cloth secured tightly to the mouth of the jar.

Set your kombucha aside to brew in a warm spot out of direct sunlight and where the air circulates. It brews best at a temperature of between 75°F and 80°F. As it brews, it will lighten in color. Taste it after 5 days. If you prefer a more sour flavor, allow the kombucha to continue to brew and taste it daily. If it tastes too sour, stop the fermentation sooner the next time you brew.

Using a funnel, drop 1 teaspoon of lemon zest into each bottle. When you pour in the kombucha, it will loosen the bits that get stuck in the funnel.

Remove the SCOBY from the jar, set it aside, and cover it to protect it from impurities.

Stir the kombucha in the jar to evenly distribute the yeast. Set aside ½ cup of kombucha to make more. Pour the remaining kombucha through the funnel into the bottles, up to but not into the necks. Close the bottles.

The bacteria and yeast in the kombucha will eat the sugars present and excrete carbon dioxide, creating carbonation. This gas can build up so much pressure that bottles explode, so to help contain possible messes, store the bottles in a cupboard or cardboard box. Burp your bottles every day or two (i.e., open them slightly) to release built-up gas. After about 2 days, move the bottles to the refrigerator. The fermentation will slow down, but it won't stop, and the drink will become less sweet and more vinegary within 2 weeks.

With your SCOBY and the reserved ½ cup kombucha, you are ready to start a new batch of kombucha.

A SCOBY Hotel

At some point, you may need a break from brewing. Your SCOBY doesn't need 24/7 care like a pet. You can put it up in a SCOBY hotel—a place for your SCOBYs to relax and take a vacation from fermenting.

To make a SCOBY hotel, prepare your tea in a large jar as usual for kombucha, then add all your SCOBYs. Cover the jar with a cloth as before and place the SCOBY hotel on a shelf or countertop. The SCOBYs can sit for several weeks, depending on your kitchen's environment. (I let mine go for about 8 weeks.) If the level of kombucha gets low in your SCOBY hotel, top it up with a bit of your current brew. When you feel ready to get back into the kombucha-brewing rhythm, remove one or two SCOBYs to start a fresh batch of kombucha.

Near the end of your SCOBYs' stay, the kombucha will taste very vinegary. Your living SCOBYs will need some food at this point in order to survive. Make a new hotel for them.

And now for your next recipe . . .

Oh no! You forgot about your kombucha while it was brewing and now it tastes too vinegary to drink. Congratulations! You haven't failed at making kombucha, you've succeeded at making great vinegar. Use some of it to make hot sauce (page 91), mustard (page 129), and other recipes that call for cider vinegar.

Sparkling Tepache

After you've cut up a fresh pineapple, get the most out of it and use merely scraps to make this fruity, bubbly, refreshing, and sweet tepache. Like many fermented foods, tepache essentially makes itself. You simply place pineapple peels, the sliced core, sugar, and water in a big jar, stir occasionally, and wait between two and five days for the concoction to bubble to life. Strain it, bottle it if desired, and serve it chilled.

Peel the pineapple, retaining 1 large piece to submerge the smaller pieces in the jar. (Save the pineapple flesh for another use.)

Place the sugar and water in a wide-mouth 1-gallon glass jar. Stir well to dissolve the sugar. Add the pineapple peels, putting the smaller pieces in first and topping with the large peel. Position a small jar on top of this large pineapple peel; the jar will push down the contents and the liquid will rise, submerging the peels and impeding mold from forming on them. To prevent impurities from finding their way into the jar, cover it with a breathable, tightly woven cloth secured tightly to the mouth of the jar. Set the jar aside at room temperature.

Stir and taste daily. The tepache will begin to bubble vigorously between 1 and 5 days. When you like the flavor, strain the tepache into clean bottles and store in the refrigerator before drinking. Save the peels for a second batch (see Note). The tepache will keep for months in the refrigerator, however, it tastes best soon after it's ready to drink. If you leave the bottles in the refrigerator, burp them every 2 weeks.

Note

As with the other recipes in this book that call for peels, choose organic pineapples, as peels contain pesticide residue.

Makes about 8 cups

1 large organic pineapple (see Note)

1 cup sugar, preferably less refined, such as brown sugar, rapadura, or jaggery

8 cups water

And now for your next recipe . . .

- Use your still-sweet peels for a second infusion and another batch of tepache. I make my second batch more concentrated, as the first infusion does reduce the amount of sugar and flavor present in the peels. After straining the first infusion, add ½ cup sugar and 4 cups water to the jar and stir well. Add the pineapple peels. Because the bacteria and yeast that reproduced in the first batch have now colonized the peels, this second infusion will ferment very quickly, often in less than a day, depending on the heat of your kitchen.

- But wait, there's more! Make scrap vinegar for a third infusion, following the instructions on page 101.

12

Low-Waste
Desserts:
All for the Cause!

Grown-Up Brownies

While I developed this recipe and offered friends and family samples, they often first asked, "Why make brownies *with sourdough*?" Some of them acted as though I needed a sourdough intervention. Others wondered what food I *wouldn't* put sourdough into. (I'm sure there is an answer to that question.) But after trying the brownies, they'd ask, "Why make brownies *without sourdough*?" followed by "Any left?"

If you like dark chocolate, you'll like these. If you like dark chocolate with a glass of red wine, you might be thinking, "Now you're talking." These brownies taste less sweet than a typical brownie, and the sourdough adds just a hint of tang. If you prefer more of a tangy flavor, allow your active, bubbly leaven to fall for a couple of hours before preparing the brownies.

Make the leaven: Between 6 and 12 hours before you plan to bake, combine the flours, water, and starter in a jar or non-reactive bowl, mix well, cover with a lid or plate, and set aside at room temperature.

Preheat the oven to 350°F and generously grease and flour a 9-inch square baking pan with butter (see Note).

Make the brownies: Slowly melt the chocolate and butter in a double boiler. (If you don't have a double boiler, fill a small pot with 2 inches of water and bring to a simmer. Place the chocolate and butter in a heatproof glass or metal bowl, and place atop—but not touching—the simmering water.) Whisk until smooth. Remove from the heat.

In a large bowl, whisk together the sugar, salt, and cocoa powder.

Add the egg and egg yolk and the vanilla, whisking until smooth. Stir in the melted chocolate. Add the leaven; because it will be thick and a little taut, it will take a few minutes to incorporate. Stir in the nuts, if desired.

Makes sixteen 2-inch brownies

For the Leaven

¼ cup (30 g) all-purpose flour

¼ cup (33 g) whole wheat or spelt flour

¼ cup (59 ml) water

2 tablespoons (30 g) active sourdough starter (page 105)

For the Brownies

1 cup plus 2 tablespoons (200 g) semisweet or bittersweet chocolate chips

All-purpose flour, for dusting the baking pan

½ cup (1 stick or 114 g) unsalted butter, plus more to grease the baking pan

⅔ cup (132 g) sugar

¾ teaspoon (5 g) salt

¼ cup (21 g) unsweetened cocoa powder

1 large egg plus 2 egg yolks

1½ teaspoons Bourbon Street Vanilla Extract (page 110) or store-bought

½ cup (54 g) chopped walnuts, toasted (optional)

recipe continues »→

Pour the batter into the prepared baking pan and smooth the top. Place the pan on the middle rack of the oven and bake for 35 to 40 minutes, until a fork inserted into the center comes out clean. Allow to cool completely on a cooling rack before cutting and serving. Store in a glass container. The brownies will keep for at least 3 days at room temperature or for several months in the freezer.

Note

Because this is a zero-waste cookbook, I do not use parchment paper to line the baking pan. Parchment does make sticky brownies easier to remove from the pan. If you use parchment, look for an unbleached, compostable brand.

SYS (Save Your Scraps)

With your leftover egg whites, you can next make coconut macaroons (page 273) in the name of food-waste avoidance. And if you don't feel like making anything right away with your egg whites, store them in the freezer, where they keep very well.

Flaky Fruit Galette

Think of a fruit galette as a learner's permit for fruit pie. If pastry intimidates you, then start with this rustic tart. Roll out the chilled pastry dough, place the prepared fruit in the center, fold the edges of the dough over the filling, leaving much of the fruit exposed, then bake and revel in the praise of your family or guests as they devour your galette.

Like the fruit crumble on page 268, this recipe works well with a variety of fruit—apples, berries, stone fruit, and so on. So, if you have fruit on hand, use that before heading to the grocery store to buy more. Make the pastry a day or two in advance, if desired.

On a well-floured surface, roll out the pastry into a 14-inch circle, about ⅛ inch thick. Place the dough on a baking sheet or in a large cast-iron pan.

In a medium bowl, toss the fruit with the lemon juice.

In a small bowl, combine the flour, sugar, cinnamon, nutmeg, and salt. Add this mixture to the fruit and toss until well combined.

Spread the fruit mixture in the center of the pastry, leaving a 2½-inch border around the edge. Gently fold the dough up and partly over the filling, overlapping and pinching to make an edge about 2 inches wide, with most of the fruit exposed in the center.

Whisk the egg and water lightly together to make an egg wash, if using. Brush the edges of the dough with it.

Chill the galette in the freezer for 10 minutes or the refrigerator for 30 minutes.

Preheat the oven to 375°F.

Bake the galette for 40 to 50 minutes, until the crust is golden brown. Cover leftovers with a large, inverted plate or bowl and store at room temperature for about 2 days.

Serves 8

1 recipe No-Fear Pastry (page 107), chilled

5 cups chopped fresh fruit

Juice of 1 lemon (about 2 tablespoons)

¼ cup (34 g) all-purpose flour

¾ cup (150 g) sugar

⅛ teaspoon ground cinnamon

⅛ teaspoon grated nutmeg

Pinch of salt

1 large egg, lightly beaten with 1 teaspoon water (optional; see Note)

Note

Omit the egg wash if you're vegan.

SYS (Save Your Scraps)

If you applied egg wash to your galette, you now have a partially beaten egg left over. If you won't use this immediately, you can freeze it in a small wide-mouth jar. When you want to use it later, perhaps in the frittata (page 207), thaw it in the refrigerator on the bottom shelf the night before you need it.

Any-Fruit Crunchy Crumble

Because you can make this dessert with various kinds of fruit you may have on hand—apples, berries, cherries, stone fruit, rhubarb, or a combination—and you don't want to waste any of that precious bounty, you almost have a duty to make and eat this. We all do what we must!

So, here is a sample game plan for this recipe in your efficient, zero-waste kitchen: Prepare a batch of nut or seed milk, set aside ¼ cup of the resulting pulp, and make this topping. Store the topping for several days in the refrigerator in a glass jar so you'll see it in there and remember you have it. When you want to quickly make the dessert, you'll have already done half the prep. Chop the fruit, place it in a dish, sprinkle on the topping, and bake.

Preheat the oven to 350°F.

In a large bowl, toss the fruit with the lemon juice, ¼ cup of the flour, and ¼ cup of the granulated sugar. Arrange the fruit in a 9-inch glass pie plate.

Combine the remaining ½ cup flour, the oats, nut or seed pulp, the remaining 2 tablespoons granulated sugar, the brown sugar, cinnamon, nutmeg, and salt in a medium bowl. Cut in the butter with a pastry blender or two knives until the topping looks crumbly. Stir in the nuts.

Sprinkle the crumble mixture on top of the fruit filling. Bake until the topping is golden, the fruit is soft, and the juices are bubbling, about 25 minutes. Cover leftovers with a large, inverted plate or bowl and store at room temperature for about 2 days.

Serves 8

5 cups chopped fresh fruit

Juice of 1 lemon
(about 2 tablespoons)

¾ cup (101 g) all-purpose flour

½ cup (54 g) old-fashioned rolled oats

¼ cup (45 g) pulp from No-Waste Nut or Seed Milk (page 112), or 2 tablespoons (13 g) almond meal

6 tablespoons (75 g) granulated sugar

¼ cup (25 g) brown sugar

⅛ teaspoon ground cinnamon

⅛ teaspoon grated nutmeg

Pinch of salt

4 tablespoons (½ stick; 57 g) unsalted butter or ¼ cup coconut oil, chilled

¼ cup (33 g) chopped toasted nuts

And now for your next recipe . . .

If you make an apple crumble, use the apple peels and cores to start a batch of scrap vinegar (page 101). When the vinegar is ready, use it to cook or to clean with, and be proud of how frugal and self-sufficient you are.

The Freshest Pumpkin Pie

Once you bake a pumpkin pie with fresh pumpkin *and* fresh ginger, you simply cannot go back—you can't untaste those flavors together. And don't be surprised if, after your family and friends taste their first bite of this pie, they appoint you as designated Thanksgiving dinner pumpkin pie baker. I feel obligated to let you know what you're getting into here.

Like many recipes in this book, you can make this pie in stages, if you prefer. Make the pumpkin purée in advance and either refrigerate or freeze it until you make the pie. Make the pastry a day or two in advance, as well—heck, freeze that, too. When you crave your pumpkin pie, assemble the parts and bake; it's like a meal kit but tastier, less expensive, and without the packaging waste.

Preheat the oven to 350°F.

Stab the top of the pumpkin a few times. Place it in a dish and bake, checking for doneness after 40 minutes. You should be able to easily slide a knife into the pumpkin. If you can't, continue to bake, checking often. (Alternatively, cook a small pumpkin in a pressure cooker following the manufacturer's instructions.)

When the pumpkin is cool enough to handle, cut off the top, cut out the core, then slice in half and remove the seeds. Peel the skin from the pumpkin flesh.

Cut the pumpkin flesh into 2-inch pieces, then run it through a food mill or purée in a food processor. You should have about 2 cups. (If desired, refrigerate for several days or freeze for several months.)

Preheat the oven to 375°F.

Serves 8

1 sugar pie pumpkin

1 recipe No-Fear Pastry (page 107), chilled

½ cup (50 g) brown sugar

1 tablespoon finely minced fresh ginger

1 teaspoon ground cinnamon

¼ teaspoon ground cloves

½ teaspoon salt

3 large eggs

½ cup (125 ml) heavy cream or half-and-half

recipe continues ⟫→

←« recipe continued from previous page

Roll the pastry into a circle about 12 inches in diameter and ⅛ inch thick. Transfer to a 9-inch pie plate, then trim the pastry to extend only ½ inch beyond the plate edge. Fold the pastry edge under itself, making it flush with the top of the pie plate. Pinch this rim with your fingers to crimp it. Place in the refrigerator to briefly chill while you make the pie filling.

With any excess pastry pieces, cut out shapes such as leaves, hearts, stars, or whatever else you like. Chill these as well on a small baking sheet or plate.

Combine the brown sugar, ginger, cinnamon, cloves, and salt in a small bowl. Lightly beat the eggs in a large bowl. Stir in the sugar mixture, then add the pumpkin purée and the cream. Combine well.

Pour the filling into the pie crust and bake until the filling is set, 50 minutes to 1 hour. Test for doneness with a knife inserted in the center; it should come out very clean.

Similarly, bake the pastry shapes for 10 to 12 minutes.

Allow the pie to cool before adding the decorative shapes and serving. Cover leftovers with an inverted plate or bowl. Store in the refrigerator for about 5 days.

And now for your next recipe . . .

A sugar pie pumpkin contains about ¾ cup of seeds, depending on size, and you can roast these seeds for a seasonal treat. Wipe off the pumpkin pulp and rinse the seeds. Pat them dry with a dish towel, then toss them in a mixture of 1 tablespoon olive oil, ½ teaspoon salt, and your desired spices, such as the chili powder on page 98. Spread out in a single layer on a baking sheet and roast at 350°F for 15 minutes. Give them a stir, then bake until golden and crunchy, about another 10 minutes.

Chocolate-Dipped Coconut Macaroons

I included this recipe as a vehicle to use up the egg whites left over from the Grown-Up Brownies (page 263). This makes 14 to 16 small macaroons, so depending on how many people you'll offer them to, you may want to double the recipe. Even if only you will eat them, you may want to do that.

You can toast the almonds for this while the oven heats up, to conserve time and energy. But if you prefer not to multitask and to bake in the moment, make the macaroons first. As they cool, toast the nuts until fragrant. After everything has cooled, melt the chocolate. You don't want it to harden before the macaroons have cooled enough to handle for dipping.

Preheat the oven to 350°F and grease a large baking sheet with butter.

In a large bowl, whisk the egg whites, sugar, and extract until frothy. Stir in the coconut and salt.

Scoop up and roll into 1-inch compact balls. Place the balls on the baking sheet. Make a dent in the top of each ball with your thumb.

Bake the macaroons until golden and firm, about 15 minutes. Let cool on the baking sheet for 10 minutes, then move them to a cooling rack. Keep the oven on.

Spread the almonds in a single layer on the baking sheet or in a cast-iron skillet. Toast for about 5 minutes. Stir and continue toasting for another 5 minutes or until fragrant.

After the macaroons have cooled, melt the chocolate in a double boiler or in a small metal bowl placed over a pot of boiling water. Remove from the heat when not quite melted. Stir until smooth.

Dip the tops of the macaroons in the chocolate. Place a roasted almond in each dent. Allow the chocolate to cool, then serve. Store in a glass jar. The macaroons will keep for at least 3 days.

Makes 14 to 16 macaroons

Butter, to grease the baking sheet

2 large egg whites

½ cup (100 g) sugar

½ teaspoon almond extract (or Bourbon Street Vanilla Extract, page 110)

2 cups (180 g) shredded unsweetened coconut

⅛ teaspoon salt

14 to 16 raw whole almonds

½ cup (89 g) semisweet or bittersweet chocolate chips

And now for your next recipe . . .

If you'd like to make some nut butter (page 130), toast a whole pile of almonds at the same time you make these macaroons. You can literally whip up a batch of nut butter in your food processor while your macaroons cool.

Mexican Hot Chocolate Bread Pudding

After you taste this rich, creamy, and crisp-on-top chocolate dessert, bread will never go to waste in your home ever again. You'll actually look forward to finding day-old bread in your kitchen. You may start asking your neighbors for a crust of bread, like an extra on the set of *Les Mis*. Or you may simply toast fresh bread just to make this (which works well).

For the bread component of this recipe, choose a sweet white French batard (it's like a much shorter, much wider baguette), Italian loaf, or quality white sandwich bread from a bakery or your oven.

Preheat the oven to 350°F. Grease a 9-inch square baking dish with a little butter.

Combine the sugar, cocoa, cinnamon, nutmeg, cayenne, and salt in a small bowl.

Pour the milk into a large saucepan over medium heat. Add the cocoa mixture and the vanilla, and cook, whisking, until everything is combined and the cocoa has dissolved, about 2 minutes. (If you stop here, you will have very delicious Mexican hot chocolate to drink.)

Off the heat, add the butter and allow it to melt. Whisk to incorporate it into the hot chocolate.

When the mixture has cooled, whisk in the eggs. (Caution: Do not skip this cooling step! Adding the eggs to hot liquid will cause them to curdle.)

Place the bread cubes in the saucepan and toss to coat evenly with the chocolate mixture. Pour the contents of the saucepan into the prepared baking dish. Sprinkle on the chocolate chips.

Bake until a knife inserted near the center comes out clean, 50 to 55 minutes. To store, cover leftovers with an inverted bowl or plate in the refrigerator. The bread pudding will keep for about 5 days.

Serves 4 to 6

¼ cup (½ stick; 57 g) unsalted butter, plus more to grease baking dish

½ cup (100 g) sugar

¼ cup (21 g) good-quality unsweetened cocoa powder

1 teaspoon ground cinnamon

½ teaspoon grated nutmeg

⅛ teaspoon cayenne pepper

Large pinch of salt

2 cups (500 ml) whole or 2% milk or No-Waste Nut or Seed Milk (page 112)

1 teaspoon Bourbon Street Vanilla Extract (page 110) or store-bought

2 large eggs, lightly beaten

5 cups (225 g) ½-inch bread cubes, from day-old white bread (see Note)

⅓ cup (60 g) semisweet or bittersweet chocolate chips

Note

If using fresh bread, spread cubes in a layer on a baking sheet, and bake at 300°F for 10 minutes to dry it out.

And now for your next recipe . . .

Grind extra bread into crumbs for the vegetable pancakes (page 172) or the kale salad (page 204).

	SUN	MON	TUES

SUN / MON / TUES

A Month of Meals:
Your Zero-Waste Chef Calendar

1

Eat-All-Your-Vegetables Pancakes *(page 172)*, Two-Ingredient Sour Cream *(page 118)*

One-Bean, One-Vegetable, One-Grain Salad *(page 206)*

Clear-out-the-fridge soup

2

Toast, Any-Nut Nut Butter *(page 130)*, fruit

One-Bean, One-Vegetable, One-Grain Salad *(page 206)*

Ricotta and Ratatouille Galette *(page 212; use the leftover ricotta for day 3)*

3

Oatmeal with toppings of your choice

Sandwich on Sourdough Bread *(page 143)*

Use-All-the-Vegetables Frittata *(page 207; add the leftover ricotta)*

8

Huevos Rancheros *(page 161)*, Restaurant-Style Refried Beans *(page 180)*, Tender and Tangy Sourdough Tortillas *(page 108)*

Ribollita *(page 225)*

Granny's Pot Pie *(page 220; if using nut/seed milk, add pulp to the granola on day 9; make extra pastry for day 10)*

9

Anything Goes Granola *(page 158)*, Yogurt Begets Yogurt *(page 115)*, fruit

Huevos Rancheros *(page 161)*, Restaurant-Style Refried Beans *(page 180)*, Tender and Tangy Sourdough Tortillas *(page 108)*

Granny's Pot Pie *(page 220)*

10

Sweet Sourdough Pancakes *(page 151)*

Freestyle savory hand pies *(use pot pie pastry)*

Black-Eyed Pea and Mushroom Burgers *(page 199; cook extra beans for day 12; save the broth)*, Lebanese Tabbouleh *(page 168)*

15

Sourdough Sticky Buns *(page 155)*

Cauliflower and Potato Dal *(page 217)*, rice

Feed-the-Flock Bean and Mushroom Shepherd's Pie *(page 193)*

16

Anything Goes Granola *(page 158)*, Yogurt Begets Yogurt *(page 115)*, fruit

Kimchi Fried Rice *(page 203)*

Feed-the-Flock Bean and Mushroom Shepherd's Pie *(page 193)*

17

Sweet Sourdough Pancakes *(page 152)*

Feed-the-Flock Bean and Mushroom Shepherd's Pie *(page 193)*

Use-All-the-Vegetables Frittata *(page 207)*

22

Huevos Rancheros *(page 161)*, Restaurant-Style Refried Beans *(page 180)*, Tender and Tangy Tortillas *(page 108)*

Sourdough Pizza with Tomato-Garlic Sauce *(page 227)*

Takeout-Style Chana Masala *(page 197)*, Dosas *(page 182)*

23

Oatmeal with toppings of your choice

Restaurant-Style Refried Beans *(page 180)*, Tender and Tangy Tortillas *(page 108)*

Takeout-Style Chana Masala *(page 197)*, Dosas *(page 182)*

24

Sweet Sourdough Pancakes *(page 152)*

Sourdough Bread *(page 143)*, Preserved Lemon Hummus *(page 248)*, roasted vegetables

Eat-All-Your-Vegetables Pancakes *(page 172)*, green salad

29

Eat-All-Your-Vegetables Pancakes *(page 172)* and Two-Ingredient Homemade Sour Cream *(page 118)*

Restaurant Leftovers

Kernel-to-Cob Corn Chowder *(page 215)*

30

Oatmeal with toppings of your choice

Chili sans Carne *(page 222)*

Black-Eyed Pea and Mushroom Burgers *(page 199)*

WEDS	THURS	FRI	SAT
4 Sweet Sourdough Pancakes *(page 151)* Leftover frittata on Sourdough Bread *(page 143)* *Leftovers Night*	**5** Toast, Any-Nut Nut Butter *(page 130)*, fruit Savory Sourdough Pancakes *(page 152)* Empamosas *(page 184)*, Farro and Kale Salad with Preserved Lemon and Dried Apricots *(page 204)*	**6** Oatmeal with toppings of your choice Sandwich on Sourdough Bread *(page 143)* Ribollita *(page 225; add the leftover kale stems and whey)*	**7** Whole Wheat Sourdough Buttermilk Waffles *(page 150)* Customizable Stir-Fry with Peanut Sauce *(page 181)* Ribollita *(page 225)*
11 Anything Goes Granola *(page 158)*, Yogurt Begets Yogurt *(page 115)*, and fruit Black-Eyed Pea and Mushroom Burgers *(page 199)*, Lebanese Tabbouleh *(page 168)* *Leftovers Night*	**12** Scrambled eggs with veggies One-Bean, One-Vegetable, One-Grain Salad *(page 206)* Frugal Fennel-Frond Pesto and Pasta *(page 209)*, steamed vegetables	**13** Sweet Sourdough Pancakes *(page 152)* One-Bean, One-Vegetable, One-Grain Salad *(page 206)* Cauliflower and Potato Dal *(page 217; cook the lentils in bean broth)*, Dosas *(page 182)*	**14** Oatmeal with toppings of your choice Roasted vegetables *(page 176; make extra for shepherd's pie)* Cauliflower and Potato Dal *(page 217)*, rice
18 Oatmeal with toppings of your choice Leftover frittata, green salad *(make extra dressing for day 20)* *Leftovers Night*	**19** Sweet Sourdough Pancakes *(page 151)* Clear-out-the-fridge soup Customizable Stir-Fry with Peanut Sauce *(page 181)*	**20** Oatmeal with toppings of your choice Customizable Stir-Fry with Peanut Sauce *(page 181)* One-Bean, One-Vegetable, One-Grain Salad *(page 206; cook extra chickpeas for the chana masala and hummus)*	**21** Whole Wheat Sourdough Buttermilk Waffles *(page 150)* Sourdough Pizza with Tomato-Garlic Sauce *(page 227)* Clear-out-the-fridge soup *(freeze leftovers for next month)*
25 Toast, Any-Nut Nut Butter *(page 130)*, fruit Dosas *(page 182)*, Sautéed Swiss Chard *(page 171)* *Leftovers Night*	**26** Sweet Sourdough Pancakes *(page 152)* Sourdough Bread *(page 143)*, Preserved Lemon Hummus *(page 248)*, Lebanese Tabbouleh *(page 168)* Chili sans Carne *(page 222)*	**27** Toast, Any-Nut Nut Butter *(page 130)*, fruit Chili sans Carne *(page 222)*, Lebanese Tabbouleh *(page 168)* Frugal Fennel-Frond Pesto and Pasta *(page 209)*, steamed vegetables	**28** Scrambled eggs with veggies Farro and Kale Salad with Preserved Lemon and Dried Apricots *(page 204)* *Out for Dinner*

Acknowledgments

I have a newfound appreciation for just how many people help bring a cookbook into this world. First, I want to thank my blog readers and social media audience for the time you've taken to read my posts and comment on them, for trying my recipes, and for following me on this zero-waste, low-waste, or whatever-you'd-like-to-call-it journey.

Thank you to Jen Knoch, for asking if I'd thought about writing a book and introducing me to my fabulous agent, Carly Watters. As for what I was hoping to do, Carly, you simply get it. Thank you for representing me and for helping turn my book into a reality. Thanks to you, I have a dream team at Penguin Random House and truly cannot believe my good fortune. Thank you to my US editor, Suzy Swartz, for your brilliant edits on the manuscript. They made all the difference. You are an absolute pleasure to work with, as are the Penguin Random House teams in the United States and Canada: Andrea Magyar, Michelle Arbus, Lucia Watson, Alyssa Adler, Roshe Anderson, Abdi Omer, Ashley Tucker, and Erica Rose. The way my photographer, Ashley McLaughlin, captured my vision has convinced me that she is telepathic.

Dozens of people tested these recipes. Thank you all for your time and helpful feedback. Rachael Edinger went above and beyond. My dedicated assistant, Cecilia Angkawidjaya, coached me across the recipe development finish line when I didn't want to spend one more minute in my kitchen. You made that last stretch so much fun.

Thank you to my writer friends and colleagues. Alice LaPlante helped me put together a book proposal and assured me my book would find a home. Rhonda Abrams encouraged me (repeatedly) to put my voice into these pages (how'd I do, Rhonda?).

Many family members helped throughout the long process of writing a cookbook. I want to thank Forest and Zora Nicola, John Glen, Amy Turcotte Doyle, Michelle Snarr, and Joan Temple. Thank you to my partner, Chandra Nicola, for constantly reassuring me that I could finish this giant project. Finally, I want to thank my children and inspiration, Mary Katherine and Charlotte Glen. With your literal good taste, you both knew exactly how to improve a dish. Thank you both for enduring me as I worked on "My Book." I could not have written it without you.

Notes

Chapter 1: Three, Two, One, Zero: Getting Started

American consumers generate, on average, 4½ pounds of trash per person every day: "Advancing Sustainable Materials Management: 2017 Fact Sheet." EPA.gov, November 2019. https://www.epa.gov/sites/production/files /2019-11/documents/2017_facts_and_figures _fact_sheet_final.pdf.

Much of this waste consists of materials we used briefly, like food packaging: Ibid.

materials we didn't use at all, like food: Milman, Oliver. "Americans Waste 150,000 Tons of Food Each Day—Equal to a Pound per Person." The Guardian, April 18, 2018. https://www.the guardian.com/environment/2018/apr/18 /americans-waste-food-fruit-vegetables-study.

A little over half of that waste ends up in landfills: "Advancing Sustainable Materials Management: 2017 Fact Sheet." EPA.gov, November 2019. https://www.epa.gov/sites/production/files /2019-11/documents/2017_facts_and_figures _fact_sheet_final.pdf.

a greenhouse gas 84 times more potent than carbon dioxide over a twenty-year period: Core Writing Team. Rep. Edited by Rajendra K. Pachauri and Leo Meyer. *Climate Change 2014 Synthesis Report*. Geneva, Switzerland: Intergovernmental Panel on Climate Change, 2014.

more **plastic than fish:** Rep. *The New Plastics Economy: Rethinking the Future of Plastics*. Cowes, UK: The Ellen MacArthur Foundation, n.d. https://www.ellenmacarthurfoundation.org/assets/ downloads/EllenMacArthurFoundation_TheNew PlasticsEconomy_Pages.pdf.

threatens plants, animals, and humans alike: Wang, Jiao, Xianhua Liu, Yang Li, Trevor Powell, Xin Wang, Guangyi Wang, and Pingping Zhang. "Microplastics as Contaminants in the Soil Environment: A Mini-Review." Edited by Jay Gan. *Science of the Total Environment* 691 (November 15, 2019): 848–57. https://doi.org /https://doi.org/10.1016/j.scitotenv.2019.07.209.

recycling rate remained steady between 2012 and 2017: "Plastics: Material-Specific Data." EPA. Environmental Protection Agency, October 30, 2019. https://www.epa.gov/facts-and-figures- about-materials-waste-and-recycling/plastics- material-specific-data.

plastic waste between 2010 and 2016: Ritchie, Hannah, and Max Roser. "Plastic Pollution." Our World in Data, September 1, 2018. https://our worldindata.org/plastic-pollution.

the world will need to bury, burn, or recycle an estimated 111 million metric tons of plastic: Brooks, Amy L., Shunli Wang, and Jenna R. Jambeck. "The Chinese Import Ban and Its Impact on Global Plastic Waste Trade." *Science Advances* 4, no. 6 (June 20, 2018). https://doi.org/10.1126/sciadv.aat0131.

These products will still end up in a landfill: Kaas Boyle, Lisa. "The Myth of the Recycling Solution." Plastic Pollution Coalition. Plastic Pollution Coalition, October 5, 2015. https://www.plastic pollutioncoalition.org/pft/2015/8/23/the-myth-of- the-recycling-solution.

coming into contact with plastic?: Trasande, Leonardo, Rachel M. Shaffer, and Sheela Sathyanarayana. "Food Additives and Child Health." *Pediatrics* 142, no. 2 (August 2018). https://doi.org/https://doi.org/10.1542/peds. 2018–1410.

child loss, cancer, and genetic disorders: "Endocrine Disruptors." National Institute of Environmental Health Sciences. U.S. Department of Health and Human Services. https://www.niehs.nih.gov /health/topics/agents/endocrine/index.cfm.

raise similar health concerns: Jacobson, Melanie H., Miriam Woodward, Wei Bao, Buyun Liu, and Leonardo Trasande. "Urinary Bisphenols and Obesity Prevalence Among U.S. Children and Adolescents." *Journal of the Endocrine Society* 3, no. 9 (July 25, 2019): 1715–26. https://doi.org /https://doi.org/10.1210/js.2019-00201.

render materials grease- and waterproof: Fassler, Joe. "The Bowls at Chipotle and Sweetgreen Are Supposed to Be Compostable. They Contain Cancer-Linked 'Forever Chemicals.'" The Counter, September 2, 2020. https://newfood economy.org/pfas-forever-chemicals-sweetgreen- chipotle-compostable-biodegradable-bowls/.

response to infections: "Perfluoroalkyl and Polyfluoroalkyl Substances (PFAS)." National Institute of Environmental Health Sciences. U.S. Department of Health and Human Services. Accessed 2020. https://www.niehs.nih.gov/health /topics/agents/pfc/index.cfm.

most food waste occurs at the consumer level: "Characterization and Management of Food Loss and Waste in North America." cec.org. Canadian Commission for Environmental Cooperation, 2017. http://www3.cec.org/islandora/en/item/11772- characterization-and-management-food-loss-and- waste-in-north-america-en.pdf.

any other stop along the supply chain: Gunders, Dana, and Jonathan Bloom. Rep. *Wasted: How America Is Losing Up to 40 Percent of Its Food from Farm* *to Fork to Landfill.* Natural Resources Defense Council, 2017. https://www.nrdc.org/sites /default/files/wasted-2017-report.pdf.

near-one pound of food per person: Milman.

food waste accounts for about 8 percent of greenhouse gas emissions: "Reduced Food Waste." Project Drawdown, July 1, 2020. https://www .drawdown.org/solutions/food/reduced-food-waste.

the aviation industry generates 2.5 percent: Penner, Joyce E., David H. Lister, David J. Griggs, David J. Dokken, and Mack McFarland. Rep. *Aviation and the Global Atmosphere*, n.d. https://archive.ipcc.ch /ipccreports/sres/aviation/index.php?idp=0.

electric vehicles *combined*: https://drawdown.org /sites/default/files/pdfs/Drawdown_Review_2020 _march10.pdf

food cravings and more: Bell, Victoria, Jorge Ferrao, Ligia Pimentel, Manuela Pintado, and Tito Fernandes. "One Health, Fermented Foods, and Gut Microbiota." *Foods* 7, no. 12 (December 3, 2018). https://doi.org/10.3390/foods7120195.

Fermented foods benefit gut health: Ibid.

Chapter 2: Cooking Like Grandma

Fresh fruit and vegetables go to waste more than other foods: Conrad, Zach, Meredith T. Niles, Deborah A. Neher, Eric D. Roy, Nicole E. Tichenor, and Lisa Jahns. "Relationship between Food Waste, Diet Quality, and Environmental Sustainability." *Plos One* 13, no. 4 (April 18, 2018). https://doi.org/10.1371/journal.pone.0195405.

producers can ship the tomatoes long distances without damaging them: Estabrook, Barry. *Tomatoland: from Harvest of Shame to Harvest of Hope.* Kansas City, MO: Andrews McMeel Publishing, 2018.

ethylene-sensitive foods: https://www.extension. iastate.edu/smallfarms/store-fresh-garden-produce -properly; https://ucsdcommunityhealth.org /wp-content/uploads/2017/09/ethylene.pdf

mushrooms, summer squash, and sweet corn: Diffley, Atina, and Jim Slama, eds. *Wholesale Success: A Farmer's Guide to Selling, Postharvest Handling and Packing Produce.* Oak Park, IL: FamilyFarmed.org, 2010.

more potent than carbon dioxide over a twenty-year period: Core Writing Team.

draw carbon dioxide out of the atmosphere: "Composting." Project Drawdown, June 29, 2020. https://drawdown.org/solutions/composting.

probiotics help alleviate symptoms of anxiety: Hilimire, Matthew R., Jordan E. Devylder, and Catherine A. Forestell. "Fermented Foods, Neuroticism, and Social Anxiety: An Interaction Model." *Psychiatry Research* 228, no. 2 (August 2015): 203–8. https://doi.org/10.1016/j.psychres .2015.04.023.

making digestion easier for our bodies: Nkhata, Smith G., Emmanuel Ayua, Elijah H. Kamau, and Jean-Bosco Shingiro. "Fermentation and Germination Improve Nutritional Value of Cereals and Legumes through Activation of Endogenous Enzymes." *Food Science & Nutrition* 6, no. 8 (October 16, 2018): 2446–58. https://doi.org/10.1002 /fsn3.846.

Chapter 3: Changing the Culture: Fermentation

Fermentation breaks these bonds to make the nutrients available: Ibid.

Niacin in yogurt: Leblanc, J.g., J.e. Laiño, M. Juarez Del Valle, V. Vannini, D. Van Sinderen, M.p. Taranto, G. Font De Valdez, G. Savoy De Giori, and F. Sesma. "B-Group Vitamin Production by Lactic Acid Bacteria—Current Knowledge and Potential Applications." *Journal of Applied Microbiology* 111, no. 6 (September 10, 2011): 1297–1309. https://doi.org/10.1111/j.1365 -2672.2011.05157.x.

In addition, riboflavin, niacin, and thiamine help convert food to energy: "Riboflavin." NIH Office of Dietary Supplements. U.S. Department of Health and Human Services. Accessed 2020. https://ods.od.nih.gov/factsheets/Riboflavin- Consumer; "Thiamin." NIH Office of Dietary Supplements. U.S. Department of Health and Human Services. Accessed 2020. https://ods.od. nih.gov/factsheets/Thiamin-Consumer/.; "Niacin." NIH Office of Dietary Supplements. U.S. Department of Health and Human Services. Accessed 2020. https://ods.od.nih.gov/factsheets /Niacin-Consumer/.

Folate helps form DNA and RNA: "Folate." NIH Office of Dietary Supplements. U.S. Department of Health and Human Services. Accessed 2020. https://ods.od.nih.gov/factsheets/Folate- Consumer/.

a smaller insulin spike: Scazzini, Francesca, Daniele Del Rio, Nicoleta Pellegrini, and Furio Brighenti. "Sourdough Bread: Starch Digestibility and Postprandial Glycemic Response." *Journal of cereal science* 49, no. 3 (May 2009): 419–21. https://doi .org/https://doi.org/10.1016/j.jcs.2008.12.008.

may benefit those with gluten intolerance: Rizzello, Carlo G., Maria De Angelis, Raffaella Di Cagno, Alessandra Camarca, Marco Silano, Ilario Losito, Massimo De Vincenzi, et al. "Highly Efficient Gluten Degradation by Lactobacilli and Fungal Proteases during Food Processing: New Perspectives for Celiac Disease." *Applied and Environmental Microbiology* 73, no. 14 (July 18, 2007): 4499–4507. https://doi.org/10.1128 /aem.00260-07.

compost the entire layer of affected vegetables: Katz, Sandor. *The Art of Fermentation: An In-Depth Exploration of Essential Concepts and Processes from Around the World.* White River Junction, VT: Chelsea Green Publishing Co, 2013.

Certain highly toxic species of *Aspergillus* mold can develop on kombucha: "Kombucha—Toxicity Alert." *Crit Path AIDS Project*, n.d.

Chapter 4: What *Can't* a Jar Do? The Tools

the average person may be eating a credit card's worth of microplastic each week: Miles, Tom. "You May Be Eating a Credit Card's Worth of Plastic Each Week: Study." Reuters. Thomson Reuters, June 12, 2019. https://www.reuters.com/article /us-environment-plastic/you-may-be-eating-a-credit-cards-worth-of-plastic-each-week-study-idUSKCN1TD009.

Fat not only tastes good: "Dietary Fats." www.heart.org, March 23, 2014. https://www.heart.org /en/healthy-living/healthy-eating/eat-smart/fats /dietary-fats.; "The Truth about Fats: the Good, the Bad, and the in-Between." *Harvard Health*, December 11, 2015. https://www.health.harvard .edu/staying-healthy/the-truth-about-fats-bad-and-good.

Keurig alone sold nearly 10 billion packs of pods in 2014: Hamblin, James. "If You Drink Coffee From Pods, You May Want to Reconsider." *The Atlantic.* Atlantic Media Company, March 2, 2015. https://www.theatlantic.com/technology/archive /2015/03/the-abominable-k-cup-coffee-pod-environment-problem/386501/.

Some aluminum coffee pods can be recycled: "Nespresso Recycling: Recyclable Coffee Pods." Nespresso USA. https://www.nespresso.com/us /en/how-to-recycle-coffee-capsules.

often wrapped in yet more plastic: Orci, Taylor. "Are Tea Bags Turning Us Into Plastic?" *The Atlantic.* Atlantic Media Company, April 8, 2013. https://www.theatlantic.com/health/archive /2013/04/are-tea-bags-turning-us-into-plastic /274482.

Chapter 5: Zero-Waste in Real Life

Americans consume 100 billion single-use plastic shopping bags every year: "100 Billion Plastic Bags Used Annually in the US." United Nations Regional Information Centre for Western Europe (UNRIC), October 19, 2013. https://archive.unric. org/en/latest-un-buzz/28776-100-billion-plastic-bags-used-annually-in-the-us.

taxing plastic bags in cities: Zeitlin, Matthew. "Do Plastic Bag Taxes or Bans Curb Waste? 400 Cities and States Tried It out." Vox. Vox, August 27, 2019. https://www.vox.com/the-highlight/2019 /8/20/20806651/plastic-bag-ban-straw-ban-tax.

Near me in San Jose: "San Jose Transportation and Environment Committee Agenda 12-03-12." San Jose, CA, November 21, 2012.

1.4 million trillion microfibers pollute the seafloor: http://storyofstuff.org/wp-content/uploads/2017 /01/Oceans-Microfibers-and-the-Outdoor-Industry.pdf

Chapter 7: You Can Make That? Staples and Scraps

Americans spend $4 billion yearly on tortillas: "Tortilla Production Industry in the US—Market Research Report." IBISWorld, February 29, 2020. https://www.ibisworld.com/united-states/market-research-reports/tortilla-production-industry/.

Soaking speeds up the cooking time: Queiroz, Keila Da Silva, Admar Costa De Oliveira, Elizabete Helbig, Soely Maria Pissini Machado Reis, and Francisco Carraro. "Soaking the Common Bean in a Domestic Preparation Reduced the Contents of Raffinose-Type Oligosaccharides but Did Not Interfere with Nutritive Value." *Journal of Nutritional Science and Vitaminology* 48, no. 4 (August 2002): 283–89. https://doi.org/10.3177/ jnsv.48.283.

Kidney beans contain the toxin phytohemagglutinin, which boiling neutralizes: "Phytohaemagglutinin." Phytohaemagglutinin—an overview | ScienceDirect Topics, n.d. https://www.sciencedirect.com/topics /agricultural-and-biological-sciences/ phytohaemagglutinin.

Chapter 9: Side Dishes You Can Commit To

Fermentation increases the digestibility: Nkhata, Smith G., Emmanuel Ayua, Elijah H. Kamau, and Jean-Bosco Shingiro. "Fermentation and Germination Improve Nutritional Value of Cereals and Legumes through Activation of Endogenous Enzymes." *Food Science & Nutrition* 6, no. 8 (October 16, 2018): 2446–58. https://doi.org/10.1002 /fsn3.846.

Chapter 10: Make Mains, Not Waste

EWG's Clean Fifteen List: "Clean Fifteen™ Conventional Produce with the Least Pesticides." Environmental Working Group. Accessed 2020. https://www.ewg.org/foodnews/clean-fifteen.php.

Chapter 11: Naked (No-Package) Snacks and Natural Sodas

Non-organic ginger: Katz, 150.

Peels contain pesticide residue: Awasthi, Mahesh D. "Chemical Treatments for the Decontamination of Brinjal Fruit from Residues of Synthetic Pyrethroids." *Pesticide Science* 17, no. 2 (April 1986): 89–92. https://doi.org/10.1002/ps.2780170204.

Index

Note: Page numbers in *italics* indicate photos.